A WEDDING IN HAITI

Also by JULIA ALVAREZ

Novels

How the García Girls Lost Their Accents
In the Time of the Butterflies
¡YO!
In the Name of Salomé
A Cafecito Story
Saving the World

Nonfiction

Something to Declare
Once Upon a Quinceañera: Coming of Age in the USA

Poetry

Homecoming: New and Collected Poems
The Other Side/El Otro Lado
The Woman I Kept to Myself

Books for Young Readers

The Secret Footprints
How Tía Lola Came to Stay
Before We Were Free
finding miracles
A Gift of Gracias: The Legend of Altagracia
The Best Gift of All: The Legend of La Vieja Belén
Return to Sender
How Tía Lola Learned to Teach
How Tía Lola Saved the Summer
How Tía Lola Ended Up Starting Over

A Wedding in Haiti

The Story of a Friendship

JULIA ALVAREZ

A Shannon Ravenel Book

ALGONQUIN BOOKS OF CHAPEL HILL   2012

A Shannon Ravenel Book

Published by
Algonquin Books of Chapel Hill
Post Office Box 2225
Chapel Hill, North Carolina 27515-2225

a division of
Workman Publishing
225 Varick Street
New York, New York 10014

Some names have been changed to protect the privacy of individuals.

The photographs in this book are credited as follows: Isaías Orozco Lang, page 3; Nicole Sánchez, page 10; Bill Eichner, pages 38, 39, 74, 82, 83, 100, 200, 216, 219; Homero, pages 54, 55, 66, 67, 69, 104, 123; Carlos Barria (Reuters), page 143; Mikaela, pages 199, 207, 210, 235; Ana Alvarez, page 173; Thony Belizaire (AFP/Getty Images), page 242. All others by the author, except for page 25, from the author's collection.

Library of Congress Cataloging-in-Publication Data
Alvarez, Julia.
    A wedding in Haiti / Julia Alvarez. — 1st ed.
        p. cm.
    "A Shannon Ravenel book."
    ISBN 978-1-61620-130-2
    1. Alvarez, Julia — Friends and associates.   2. Alvarez, Julia —
    Travel — Haiti.   3. Authors, Dominican American — 21st century —
    Biography.   4. Haitians — Dominican Republic — Biography.
    I. Title.
    PS3551.L845A3 2012
    818'.5403 — dc23   2012000452

10 9 8 7 6 5 4 3 2 1
First Edition

for

los pitouses

&

all the Ludys

Author's Note

In telling this story, I am not claiming to be an authority on Haitian matters. This is a book about a friendship with a young Haitian, Piti, who happened into a farm and literacy project my husband and I set up in my native country, the Dominican Republic. Through that friendship has come an opportunity to discover my neighbor country, who was and still is "the sister I hardly knew." But these two journeys to Haiti are only the beginning of an evolving relationship, which has deepened with the writing of this book. My friendship with Piti and Eseline and little Ludy and their extended families and friends back in Haiti also continues to evolve and teach me how much is possible when we step outside the boundaries that separate us one from the other.

> Julia Alvarez
> September 2009 – October 2011
> *con la Altagracia a mi lado*

A WEDDING IN HAITI

ONE

Going to Piti's Wedding
in Haiti

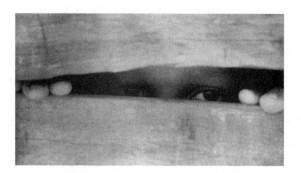

Circa 2001, the mountains of the Dominican Republic

M Y husband and I have an ongoing debate about how
old Piti was when we first met him. I say Piti was
seventeen at the most. My husband claims he was older,
maybe nineteen, even possibly twenty. Piti himself isn't
sure what year we met him. But he has been working in
the mountains of the Dominican Republic since he first
crossed the border from Haiti in 2001 when he was seventeen years old.

Bill and I might have forgotten the year, but we distinctly remember the first time we met Piti. It was late
afternoon, and we were driving past the barracks-type
housing where he lived with half a dozen other Haitian
workers on a neighboring farm. On the concrete apron in

front, the group was horsing around, like young people having fun all over the world. Piti, whose name in Kreyòl means "little one," was the smallest of the group, short and slender with the round face of a boy. He was putting the finishing touches on a small kite he was making.

I asked Bill to stop the pickup, as I hadn't seen one of these homemade *chichiguas* since I was a child. I tried to explain this to Piti, who at that point didn't understand much Spanish. His response was to grin and offer me his kite. I declined and asked if I could take his picture instead.

On the next trip, I made a point of finding Piti so I could give him the photo in the small album I'd brought as a gift. You'd have thought I was giving him the keys to a new motorcycle. He kept glancing at the photo, grinning and repeating, "Piti, Piti!" as if to convince himself that he was the boy in the photo. Or maybe he was saying thank you. *"Mèsi, mèsi"* can sound like "Piti, Piti," to an ear unused to Kreyòl.

A friendship began. Every trip I sought him out, brought him a shirt, a pair of jeans, a bag in which to cart his belongings back and forth on his periodic and dangerous crossings of the border.

What I felt toward the boy was unaccountably maternal. Somewhere in Haiti, a mother had sent her young

son to the wealthier neighbor country to help the impoverished family. Maybe this very moment she was praying that her boy be safe, earn good money, encounter kind
people. Every time I spotted the grinning boy with worried eyes, I felt the pressure of that mother's prayer in my
own eyes. Tears would spring up and a big feeling fill my
heart. Who knows why we fall in love with people who
are nothing to us?

A coffee farm or a mistress?

Over the years, Bill and I got to see a lot of Piti. Whenever we could get away from our lives and jobs in
Vermont — short trips of a week, longer trips of a few
weeks — we headed for the Dominican mountains. We
had become coffee farmers.

Every time I get started on this story, the curtain rises
on that vaudeville act that long-term couples fall into: who
did what first and how did we get in this fix.

It began in 1997 with a writing assignment for the
Nature Conservancy. I was asked to visit the Cordillera
Central, the central mountain range that runs diagonally
across the island, and write a story about anything that
caught my interest. While there, Bill and I met a group

of impoverished coffee farmers who were struggling to survive on their small plots. They asked if we would help them.

We both said of course we'd help. I meant help as in: I'd write a terrific article that would bring advocates to their cause. Bill meant help, as in roll-up-your-sleeves and *really* help. I should have seen it coming. Having grown up in rural Nebraska with firsthand experience of the disappearance of family farms, Bill has a soft spot in his heart for small farmers.

We ended up buying up deforested land and joining their efforts to grow coffee the traditional way, under shade trees, organically by default. (Who could afford pesticides?) We also agreed to help find a decent market for our pooled coffee under the name Alta Gracia, as we called our sixty, then a hundred, and then, at final count, two hundred and sixty acres of now reforested land. I keep saying "we," but, of course, I mean the marital "we," as in my stubborn beloved announces we are going to be coffee farmers in the Dominican Republic, and I say, "But, honey, how can we? We live in Vermont!"

Of course, I fell in with Don Honey, as the locals started calling Bill, when they kept hearing me calling him "honey, this," "honey, that." The jokey way I explained our decision to my baffled family and friends was that it was either a coffee farm or a mistress. Over the years, I admit, I've had moments when I wondered if a mistress might not have been easier.

We were naïve — yes, now the "we" includes both of us: We hired a series of bad farm managers. We left money in the wrong hands for payrolls never paid. One manager was a drunk who had a local mistress and used the payroll to pay everyone in her family, whether they worked on the farm or not. Another, a Seventh-Day Adventist, who we thought would be safe because he wouldn't drink or steal or have a mistress, proved to be bossy and lazy. He was *el capataz*, he boasted to his underlings, the *jefe*, the foreman. He didn't have to work. Every day turned out to be a sabbath for him. His hands should have been a tip-off, pink-palmed with buffed nails. Another manager left for New York on a visa I helped him get. (Like I said, it takes two fools to try to run a coffee farm from another country.)

Still, if given the choice, I would probably do it again. As I've told Bill many a time — and this gets me in trouble — even if in the end we're going to be royally taken, I'd still rather put my check mark on the side of light. Otherwise, all the way to being proved right, I'd have turned into the kind of cynic who has opted for a smaller version of her life.

And things have slowly improved on the mountain.

Over the years, the quality of the coffee being grown in the area has gotten better. Local farmers are being paid the Fair Trade price or higher, and the land is being farmed organically. We also started a school on our own farm after we discovered that none of our neighbors, adults or children, could read or write. It helps that I'm associated with a college, with ready access to a pool of young people eager to help. Every year, for a small stipend, a graduating senior signs on to be the volunteer teacher. Recently, we added a second volunteer to focus on community projects and help out with the literacy effort.

During the tenure of one of the better managers, Piti was hired to work on the farm. It happened while we were stateside, and when we arrived, what a wonderful surprise to find him at our door. *"Soy de ustedes."* I am yours. "No, no, no," we protested. We are the ones in your debt for coming to work at Alta Gracia.

Piti later told me how it had happened. His Haitian friend Pablo had found work on a farm belonging to some *Americanos.* (Because I'm white, married to a gringo, and living in Vermont, I'm considered American.) It was a good place: decent accommodations, reasonable hours, Fair Trade wages "even for Haitians." Piti put two and two together. The *chichigua* lady and Don Honey. We were not in country at the time, so Piti applied to the foreman, who took one look at this runt of a guy and shook his head. Piti offered to work the day, and, if at the end, he hadn't done as much clearing as the other fellows on the crew, he didn't have to be paid.

Piti turned out to be such a good worker that he became a regular. His reputation spread. After several years at Alta Gracia, he was offered a job as a foreman at a farm down the road. Piti had become a *capataz*! One with calloused hands and cracked fingernails who could outwork any man, Haitian or Dominican.

He was also a lot of fun. Nights when we were on the farm, it was open house at our little casita. Whoever was around sat down to eat supper with us. Afterward came the entertainment. At some point, a visiting student taught Piti and Pablo to play the guitar, then gave it to them. A youth group left a second guitar. Bill and I bought a third. Then, like young people all over the world, Piti and Pablo and two other Haitian friends formed a band. Mostly they sang hymns for their evangelical church. Beautiful, plaintive gospel songs à la "Amazing Grace," in which the down-and-out meet Jesus, and the rest is grace. We'd all sing along, and invariably, Bill and I would look at each other, teary-eyed, and smile.

And so, the curtain falls on the coffee-farm vaudeville act.

It was on one of those evenings that I promised Piti I'd be there on his wedding day. A far-off event, it seemed, since the boy was then only twenty, at most, and looked fifteen. One of those big-hearted promises you make that you never think you'll be called on to deliver someday.

Early August 2009, Weybridge, Vermont

The new volunteer on the farm, Eli, calls us. Piti needs to talk to us. Can we please call him? These messages are always about money: someone's mother is sick; someone needs a loan to buy tools, food, medicines, a motorcycle; to get back to Haiti for a birth, a funeral, or in this case, a wedding.

I had heard rumors. On one of his trips back home, Piti had gotten his girlfriend pregnant. (Piti had a girl-friend!) I had assumed the marriage had already taken place and that Piti had either forgotten to mention it or had thoughtfully decided not to inconvenience us by reminding me of my offer. There has to be an expiration date on grand promises.

When I call the number, Piti is giggly with good news. The baby was born back in April. Piti is leaving for Haiti within days to meet his infant daughter and to marry the mother, Eseline, on August 20. Will my husband and I be coming?

This is short notice indeed. And very inconvenient. In fact, the very week of the wedding, I'm scheduled to be at a five-day gathering of the International Council of Thirteen Indigenous Grandmothers. A Latina friend told me about the group and urged me to attend the conference. She and a contingent of her Latina friends are going. (This is during the height of the Sotomayor hearings, when the term *wise Latina* has gone to some of our heads.) I'm ripe for such a gathering. I need to connect with wise elders. As both my parents continue their decline into Alzheimer's, I've become the parent of my parents. I need an infusion of grandmotherly wisdom as I transition into being an elder myself. In addition, my registration has been paid, and there is a penalty for canceling.

"*Ay*, Piti, I'm so sorry. I can't," I try explaining.

But now there's a pebble in my shoe, even at night when I'm barefoot in bed. I go back and forth in a tizzy of indecisiveness. I pile up the reasons against changing my plans, a long list that includes the grandmothers, the conference cancellation penalty, the penalty to change my plane ticket, and more importantly, the lost opportunity for psychic help on the caretaking road ahead. On the pro side is Piti's round, boyish face, grinning at my long-ago promise that I'd be at his wedding. Sometimes a conscience is an inconvenient thing to have, and costly. But not to follow it exacts an even greater cost, having to live with the hobbled person you become when you ignore it.

Getting there from here

In a subsequent phone call, I ask Piti where in Haiti his wedding will take place. "You go almost to Port-de-Paix," he explains.

On the map, Port-de-Paix is clear across northern Haiti as the crow flies, but unfortunately, there are no direct roads there. Piti can't take us there, because he himself will have left for home before our arrival in order to make preparations for the wedding.

I e-mail my friend Madison Smartt Bell, who has written extensively about Haiti and whom I consider an authority on all things Haitian. Does he have any suggestions on how to get there from here? Madison says our best bet is to hire a guide. He recommends one based in Cap-Haïtien with the reassuring name of Handy. But Handy's English e-mails are not only not handy, they're incomprehensible. *A large Bonsor especial for you and your husband,* one of them reads. *Now I just write you for a great Remerciment especial . . . Please I am still the only for you an answer of your compreansion your answer please thank you please?*

My husband, whose Spanish is only a little better than Handy's English, suggests I call Piti back and just ask for his address in Haiti. "We'll find him," Bill says confidently.

Piti laughs outright when I put the question to him. "An address? It is not possible that way." A comment that shakes my confidence, always in much shorter supply than my husband's.

But Piti comes up with his own solution. A Haitian friend who has been working with him in the Dominican Republic is from the same area in rural Haiti. Leonardo hasn't been back home in two years, but for a fee and his return passage (he's undocumented so he will have to pay a *buscón* to smuggle him back across the border), he'll take us right to Piti's doorstep.

Leonardo turns out to be a young man of about twenty who looks like a rap star, with a big silver crucifix blazoned on his black T-shirt, mirror sunglasses, a cocky smirk, and a thick chain with a Che Guevara medallion. (Leonardo isn't sure whose image it is but guesses a famous rapper.) This tough guy appearance makes me a little wary at first, until I find out that along with his small suitcase, Leonardo is bringing a box full of spaghetti for his mother.

Midway on the trip, we're to pick up Piti's old friend, Pablo, who is already in Haiti visiting his own family. ("He'll be waiting for you at the gas station," Piti has told Leonardo.) Also along for the adventure is a Dominican friend who works as a coffee researcher for an agroforestry institute run by the government. Homero, another promising name, is curious about everything. What he doesn't know, he'll go out of his way to find out. Which is why he wants to go with us. "Haiti is like a brother I've never gotten to know."

I agree with Homero. Except for a brief trip to Port-au-Prince with my aunt and uncle twenty-five years ago, I've never set foot next door. Haiti is like a sister I've never gotten to know.

Our volunteer from Middlebury, Eli, asks if he can

join us. He only just arrived in the DR three weeks ago, and I, anyhow, am a little worried about how he will fare in the year ahead. To begin with, Eli is a redhead with fair skin, a challenging complexion type in the tropics; and we are that much closer to the sun's burning rays on our mountaintop. Eli also comes with an incredible résumé: head of the student government at Middlebury, a year's teaching position at a prestigious private school, a just-completed masters in Spanish in Madrid. But those same spiffy achievement skills might prove a handicap in a remote farming village where male ambition is pretty much confined to cockfights and mistresses.

"So you really want to spend a year on a coffee farm with no electricity, no hot water, sometimes no water at all, no Internet, no museums, cafés, restaurants, movie theaters?" Bill had asked during a phone interview while Eli was still in Spain. The guy had said "Yes"! We had to pinch ourselves in Vermont. Mid-September, Eli will be returning stateside to take his Law School Admission Test (LSAT) for law school. At one point during the trip, I pick up his heavy backpack and joke, "What have you got in here?" Sheepishly, Eli admits he brought along his thick book of LSAT exams. Our first evening in the Haitian countryside, in the waning light, I'll catch Eli sitting under a mango tree taking a practice exam. By the trip's end, I'll have no doubts at all: Eli will do just fine this year at Alta Gracia.

August 18, Santiago, Dominican Republic; los pitouses

We arrive in Santiago the night before we're to set out. All flights are on time, no cancellations or delays. A good thing because in order to be at the wedding two days from now, we have to get up at dawn tomorrow to make the journey to Piti's in one day.

Eli and Leonardo are already waiting for us when we get in from the airport. We're all spending the night at my parents' house; then at dawn, Homero will join us, and we'll be off, picking up Pablo at his gas station, and on to Piti's.

Because we get in so late, I don't bother waking my parents, already asleep in their bedroom. The night nurse slips out to give me her report: both had a good day, both ate well, both played a little dominoes — a compromised game with slippery rules, and a single objective: letting my mother win. Losing can throw a pall over the rest of her day, long after she has forgotten having played dominoes in the first place.

She has also forgotten that she no longer lives in New

York. In 2002, after forty-three years in the United States, my parents decided to move back "home," and just in time. Within the year, my father's erratic behavior and faltering memory were diagnosed as Alzheimer's. My mother followed soon thereafter.

Since the Dominican Republic is a country without institutionalized elder care, we four daughters have had to cobble together our own facility. My older sister has virtually moved down there to help run what amounts to a small business, with a social worker, Vicenta, to oversee a staff that includes a cook, a chauffeur, a person to clean the house, two gardeners, a night watchman, a night nurse, and a three-person replacement weekend crew. Good thing my parents have the resources to pay for what is not cheap care if you do it right: a decent hourly wage, an eight-hour workday, a five-day workweek, two week's paid vacation, and health insurance for employees and their large families. All those enlightened concepts their daughters were taught in good schools their money also paid for.

Good thing also that they had this house to come back to. Actually, the house was my father's idea, built with his money. My mother was dead set against it. I imagine a vaudeville act not unlike Bill's and mine over the coffee farm. It was the early seventies; we were living in the States with no plans to move back. We didn't need another house, my mother argued. But my father went ahead with his dream house. And since my mother had washed her hands of it, he didn't have to rein in any of his wild ideas. He ordered a windmill. (He loved the scene of Don Quixote tussling with one.) Inside, he housed his grow, ing library on shelves you could access as you went up the winding stairwell. Since he also loved birds, he dug out a hollow on the hillside for a sanctuary, covered with a netted structure. Underneath, he planted trees and vines, special varieties that bore fruits the birds liked. A water, fall splashed down into the sanctuary, and the waters ran through it, then were pumped back up to the top of the falls by the windmill.

My sisters and I had theories about the house. Built on a hillside for all to see, it was Papi's way of showing off to Mami's family that he had made it on his own. He had proved himself worthy of my mother's hand, after all.

Theirs had been a legendary love. As a young medical student in Santiago, my father had joined un underground group of classmates who were disaffected with the dicta, torship. Unfortunately, the group's revolutionary agenda never evolved beyond the level of a schoolboy prank: strewing nails on the dictator's motorcade route from the capital to Santiago. It was a naïveté some members paid for dearly with their lives, but my father managed to flee. He arrived in New York City in 1939, thinking he could get a job. Of course, no hospital would recognize his Dominican medical degree.

He decided to head for Canada, where he'd heard some Dominican doctors had found work. By then, he had forty-five dollars left in his pocket. On the train, he met a Canadian who asked if my father wanted to see the country and earn some money while doing so. It turned out the man owned a logging camp, a remote operation of fifteen-hundred men up near Hudson Bay. He was looking for a resident doctor for the winter. The owner didn't care where my father had gotten his degree, just as long as he could set a broken limb or tourniquet a slashed arm. My father accepted on the spot.

How this was a way of seeing Canada, I don't know. It still gives me a pang to think of him, a young man with no experience of northern winters, taking off to such a cold, desolate place. But my father always considered himself a fortunate man. "My friends in Canada call me McAlvarez, because they say I have the luck of the Irish," he used to brag, laughing. Just counting the number of times he barely escaped death at the hands of the dictatorship, I'd have to agree with them.

After the snows melted, my father collected his salary (less than he had been promised) and settled in Montreal, where he took night courses at the medical school, while also working full-time during the day. Over the next eight years, Papi managed to reearn his medical degree, at one point selling his blood to pay for his credits. (The stories were marched out whenever any of his daughters brought home a report card with a grade lower than an A.) Papi became fluent in French, and had girlfriends we sometimes heard about when Mami was out of earshot or he'd had too much to drink.

During his time in Canada, Papi took a trip to New York City to attend to a dying nephew, who'd been brought to the States in a desperate attempt to save his life. While there, my father was invited to a party, thrown by a distant cousin who fixed him up with her best friend, my mother, who was then on a shopping trip with her parents. They happened upon each other at several subsequent gatherings. By the time she had to return home, and he to Canada, they were both smitten.

During the ensuing separation, they wrote to each other every day, long letters, supplemented by cards, phone calls, telegrams. At some point, they began using a pet name for each other, *pitou*, which my father had picked up in Canada — from one of those girlfriends, I suppose.

Initially, my mother's parents did not approve of my

father. They were from the oligarchy, people who could afford shopping trips to New York. Papi was a struggling doctor, his foreign degree considered second-rate, however subsequently beefed up by his Canadian credentials. He would not be able to give my mother the lifestyle she was used to. Furthermore, Mami was ten years younger, a beauty who turned heads wherever she went. The dictator's son was said to be after her — perhaps that's why she had been whisked away to the States on a shopping trip. "Are you Katharine Hepburn?" she was often asked on New York City streets. Not that Papi was any slouch in the looks department. Those Canadian girlfriends didn't call him *pitou* for nothing.

My grandparents had hoped that distance would snuff out the romance. But it just served to stoke the young couple's determination and ardor. There was no keeping apart *los pitouses*, as they soon came to be known in the family. My grandfather finally relented and gave his approval, my grandmother reluctantly complying. My parents were married in New York City and set up housekeeping there. Soon after my sister and I were born, my grandmother began lobbying for the family to move back, where my mother's parents and their money could help fill in the financial gaps.

Although the dictatorship was still in place, my grandparents reported that the regime was loosening up. Elections were being scheduled, and a general amnesty was being extended to all exiles to return home and help build a new democracy. My father was not fooled; at least he claimed not to have been when he recounted the story to his grown daughters years later. This was a ploy by the dictator trying to ingratiate himself with the Americans who were putting pressure on him to liberalize his rule.

But Papi ended up caving in. My mother was homesick, overwhelmed with taking care of two babies, eleven months apart, with no servants to help out. Once back, my father discovered that nothing much had changed. Again, he reconnected with the underground. By the time I was ten, he was up to his ears in an imminent plot, which was cracked by the Secret Police. What saved us was a CIA contact who had promised to provide guns to the plotters. He managed to get my father, his wife, and four daughters out just in time. Four months after we left, the Mirabal sisters, who had founded the underground movement, were killed by the dictator's henchmen.

Those first years back in New York, our family scraped by on handouts from my grandparents. Eventually, my father was able to renew his license and open a practice in Brooklyn. He worked seven days a week, getting up at four thirty, leaving the house by five thirty, before the sun had come up, returning after nine at night. He scrimped and saved wherever he could. I recall how he'd take the Queensboro Bridge when he had to drive into the city to avoid paying the dollar toll through the Midtown Tunnel. Then, twice a year, he went down to his house in Santiago and lived for a week like a rich man.

My mother was finally won over. By then, our once-lone house on the Cerros de Gurabo, the hills outside Santiago, was surrounded. The area had become an exclusive suburb of McMansions. Ours was now the oldest, and a poor relation to the others. After all, the things that had made the place so grand had been the imaginative accents: the waterfall; the sanctuary; the windmill where my father, dressed in a kind of monk's robe, liked to climb to the little balcony on top to get inspired. He had started writing books on odd subjects: how to learn Chinese as a Dominican; how to be happy in old age (keep active, always have a project, write books, learn languages, play dominoes). He also wrote about his travels to an imaginary planet named Alfa Calendar, where all the problems that were now doing us in on earth had been resolved. (No wars, no poverty, plenty of windmills, nifty solar-powered belts to strap on and fly to your destination.)

Now, forty years later, the house has become their refuge. Shabby genteel is how I'd describe its current condition. Without constant maintenance and the infusion of funds, the tropics can do a number on buildings and gardens. Ceilings have begun to crack; a retainer wall has crumbled; one corner of the second floor tilts slightly; the plumbing is iffy. The birds have all died. The waterfall no longer works. Inside the windmill, the rats have helped themselves to my father's library. One small blessing of Papi's condition is that he is no longer cognizant enough to understand what has happened to his dream house.

Before I head for my bedroom, I peek in on them. They are fast asleep, holding hands as they always do across their joined hospital beds. Sometimes, Papi will wake up in the middle of the night calling out, "Pitou? Pitou?" I'll hear Mami singing lullabies to him, as those seem to be the only songs she remembers anymore.

I try to fall asleep but the weariness after a day of travel, the excitement and uncertainty about what lies ahead, compounded by my worries, keep me up for hours. (How will we know what gas station Pablo will be waiting at? How will all six of us fit in Bill's new pickup? What if we can't find Piti's house in time for the wedding?) When the alarm rings, it's still dark outside, and I've driven almost to Port-de-Paix so many times in my head that it seems unnecessary to have to get up after so little sleep and actually drive there again in person.

August 19, from Santiago to Moustique

The border crossing

We wake up at quarter to five in the morning so we can be on the road by six. It's a two-and-a-half- to three-hour drive to Dajabón, the Dominican border town, another hour to Cap-Haïtien, and then, it's anyone's guess how long the drive will be to wherever near Port-de-Paix Piti's family lives.

Before our arrival in Santiago, I had asked Vicenta to pack a box with snacks and water, precautionary supplies to which she has added a cooler with cheese, ice, boxed juices, and even a bottle of wine. These go in the flatbed of the pickup, along with our backpacks and suitcases, the box of spaghetti, some tarps in case it rains. Inside the cab, Eli, Homero, and Leonardo are crammed in the backseat, Bill and I in front.

As we drive west to Dajabón, the sun rises behind us. Since Bill and I landed last night in the dark, it's a bit of a shock to go from yesterday's serene green hillsides of Vermont to the bright, jazzy colors and noisy clutter of the Dominican countryside. We're all chatty, elated by the idea of the trip, the happy occasion of a wedding, the thrill of not knowing what we are going to find.

But as we near the border, we quiet down. Although

it doesn't get the attention of, say, the Middle East, there is a troubled history between the two small countries occupying this island. From time to time, these tensions have erupted in violence, most shamefully in 1937, when four to forty-thousand Haitians (the figures vary wildly) who were then living just this side of the Dominican border were massacred over the course of a few days. The massacre was the brainchild of Trujillo, who had the military use machetes to make it look like a grassroots uprising by farmers protecting their land from Haitian invaders.

Since then, relations between the two countries have never again erupted into outright violence. But conflicts persist, as undocumented Haitians cross over into their comparatively richer neighbor country, willing to do work Dominicans won't do, often underpaid and poorly treated, a situation not unlike Mexicans who come to El Norte in search of a better life.

The border doesn't open until nine, so we wait around for the officials to arrive to get our documents stamped and our fees paid. The first to come into the cinder-block building is a tall, plump official who takes one look at our pickup's documents and starts shaking his head. The papers are incomplete, he explains. For us to be able to enter our vehicle into Haiti, we'll need two more documents that we can only get in the capital (a five-hour drive away). In addition, the one document we do have is missing its stamps.

Bill and I raise an outcry. The wedding is *tomorrow*! We need to get there today! Besides, Homero, who made the inquiries, and my parents' driver, who ran the errand, were assured that we only needed this one document. If it required stamps, their branch office in Santiago should have stamped it. So why should we be punished for their incompetence?

The official keeps shaking his head. He is very sorry, but there is nothing he can do. We can go into Haiti by showing our passports and paying the exit fee. But the pickup, a seemingly more valuable asset than the five lives within it, will have to stay behind. We may leave it parked in their yard for a fee, of course.

I can read the signs of an impending outburst on my beloved's face, complete with an indignant rant on the bureaucratic nightmare of getting anything done in this country. We've faced it time and again trying to run the farm — a costly permit to cut down a few decaying pine trees, even though we've planted several hundred healthy shade trees to replace them; a titling process still incomplete after fourteen years. But this is no time to read the guy the riot act. There are smaller fish to fry here, and fortunately, our Dominican friend is along to show us how.

Homero begins by acknowledging that the official is right. A mistake has been made by someone else. But these Americanos have come all the way from the United States, as they are the godparents of this wedding that will take place tomorrow. Isn't there a way to resolve this little problem here now?

The official keeps shaking his head, but it's as if Homero has uttered the magic words. Suddenly we are following the official out to the yard to talk to his immediate superior, a tall, lean man with several gleaming gold teeth that give him a sinister smile. He also shakes his head while carrying our incomplete documents to his superior, another plump official with a clipboard, who shakes his head as well. But somehow in the midst of all this head shaking, six hundred pesos exchange hands (about seventeen US dollars). Before we know it, the paperwork is in order, our fees are paid, and we're all back in the pickup, not yet daring to high-five each other for fear we'll be punished for our glee and charged a further penalty.

Throughout this transaction, I'm intrigued by this ongoing visual refusal to budge (the head-shaking) coupled with the surreptitious acceptance of a bribe. It's as if it were all a performance for hidden cameras monitoring the border, cameras that will capture only what's going on from the shoulders up. At six hundred pesos, the bribe is ridiculously cheap compared to Homero's visa to enter Haiti, which cost him the equivalent of eighty-five dollars — documents nobody bothers to check. Leonardo gets off the cheapest, as he has no documents, so technically, he doesn't even exist. When I worry that without any proof, Haiti might not let him in, Leonardo smirks.

"It's my country."

"But how can the guards tell you're Haitian, if you don't have a passport?"

"They can tell," Leonardo assures me.

He's too young to know that during the massacre, Trujillo's henchmen actually had trouble telling Haitians and Dominicans apart. So they devised a test. A sprig of parsley was held up for identification: *perejil* in Spanish. But the Haitians, whose Kreyòl uses a wide, flat *r*, could not pronounce the trilled *r* in the Spanish word. Whoever mispronounced the word was slaughtered on the spot. But it's not a story I want to tell Leonardo, not now on the way to a wedding, when we are going against the currents of history, headed — so I hope — in a new direction.

The tall gates on the Dominican side open, and slowly we drive across the bridge, over the nearly dry Massacre River. Although many Dominicans believe the name came from the 1937 massacre, the river actually was christened in the eighteenth century after an especially bloody battle between the Spanish soldiers and French buccaneers. Now the river is full of women washing clothes or bathing themselves and their children.

On the Haitian side of the bridge, a white guard with a UN logo on his helmet peers into our pickup. The United Nations multinational mission has been a presence here since the last coup in 2004, replacing the Haitian army, which had already been disbanded. The soldier nods, the gates part, and just like that, we're in Haiti, and free to proceed. No red tape, no need to wheedle our way in. Haiti will take us without blinking an eye or checking our documents.

I glance out the back window, feeling a pang like the biblical Ruth leaving behind her native land, as the gates close on the Dominican side.

To Limbé and Ennery, and the meeting with Pablo

The first city on the Haitian side is Ouanaminthe, a name so rich in vowels that I half expect those luxuriant sounds to spill over in wide avenues, verandas with bougainvillea pouring over trellises, ladies with parasols parading their finery.

But Ouanaminthe is a hot, dusty town of wooden huts lining the road, punctuated by the occasional concrete house—not unlike any number of towns on the other side. "It looks like the Dominican Republic," I keep saying.

The road from Ouanaminthe to Cap-Haïtien is actually a very good one. We speed along, congratulating each other on our escapade at the border, and teasing Homero on his skill at bribery. *"Lamentablemente,"* he acknowledges, this is the way business is often done in the DR. He shares a story of visiting a national park recently with his young son, a boy of ten. No one was at the entrance gate to sell them tickets, so Homero and his son drove in, parked, and began their hike. A guard came running after them. He informed them that they had to drive back to the entrance and purchase their tickets. Homero explained that no one had been at the booth to sell them tickets. Well, then, father and son would have to come back another day, the guard persisted.

Again Homero used the magic words, "Isn't there a way we can resolve this little problem here now?" Homero ended up paying the guard less than half the amount he would have paid for their two tickets. Homero's son was shocked. "Papi, you corrupted a guard!" My glee dissipates, imagining that moment when a child's fairy-tale vision of the world begins to crack.

As we near Cap-Haïtien, we rely on Leonardo to tell us where to turn. The map shows there is a bypass we can take, southwest to Limbé, where we'll pick up Route 1. But unfortunately, Leonardo has only traveled back and forth on crowded buses or packed in the flatbed of a truck with two dozen migrating Haitians. At every crossroads, we have to stop so he can ask in Kreyòl where we can pick up Route 1. But calling what we're looking for by its official name doesn't work as well as calling it "the road to Limbé," though sometimes the answers go in opposite directions. We might as well be asking, "How do we get to the gas station where Pablo is waiting for us?" It would probably get us better results.

How *do* we find the gas station where Pablo is waiting? Once we're reasonably sure we're on Route 1 and headed for Limbé, we start worrying about our rendezvous. Leonardo actually has a phone number for Pablo; the problem is that none of our Dominican cell phones seem to work in Haiti. But just then, as if a deus ex machina had been paid under the table to intervene on our behalf, we find ourselves driving past a large gas station. Surely, they will have a phone we can use.

We pull in, but unbelievably, there is no phone at the gas station. "So how do they order their gas? By passenger pigeon?" Bill quips testily. Thank goodness none of the attendants seem to understand English.

News spreads fast, and before we know it, a young man hurries over to the pickup carrying a cordless handset with a receiver: a roving phone booth, as it were. He dials the number himself and — it seems miraculous given this setup — Pablo answers! He's already at the gas station past Ennery, waiting for us.

Again, we're elated. Things are going to work out, after all. And maybe it's the fact that he is already waiting for us that leads us to think that Ennery can't be that far away. Leonardo guesses about an hour. Try three and a half hours on very bad roads full of what Bill calls craters, not potholes. No quaint towns or roadside stands or eating places break up our tediously slow, nerve-racking progress. The mountainous road is deserted except for the occasional bus packed with travelers or huge trucks carting fuel and supplies, all coming in the opposite direction, as if they know better than to be heading where we are going.

Like a kid on a long car trip, I keep asking, "Are we almost there?" Leonardo's answers downgrade from smirking affirmations to gee-whiz shrugs, as if the roads in Haiti have been shuffled around in the two years since he has been gone.

But finally, we arrive at the station to find Pablo standing in front, holding a hanging bag to protect the suit he will wear to the wedding. Even without the hanging bag, the tall, handsome Pablo would stand out. My older sister, who is old enough to be his grandmother and still flirts with him, says Pablo is good-looking and knows it. He's also a sweetheart of a guy. Tall, lanky, with long ropey arms, Pablo actually reminds me of Bill—that is if Bill were forty years younger, black, and not as stubborn.

I can see why I need not have worried over which gas station we would meet up in, because this is the only station we've encountered since we left Limbé hours ago. The station seems to be a hub: buses stop here; motorcycle taxis wait to give travelers a ride out to their rural houses. Several businesses flank the pumps, but it's hard to tell what transaction takes place within them, as none of them have signs. They're also closed, though it's well past the noon lunch hour. The only thing open is the restaurant, but it, too, is deserted. No promising centerpieces of salt and pepper, no menus posted on the wall. There is a restroom, which does the job of eliminating any desire to eat here anyway. The toilet hasn't been flushed in ages, and there's no water at the small sink, which explains the big barrel of standing water by the door.

Out in the restaurant, a young woman stands at a counter watching us. Behind her, there is a kitchen area with empty shelves. Perhaps all the food got cooked up at noon. There seems to be nothing to order except a Haitian beer named Prestige.

"It tastes a lot like Presidente," Bill says, comparing it to the popular Dominican beer. The names also strike me as similar: Prestige, Presidente. Maybe both beer companies used the same advertising firm, specializing in developing markets in the Third World. A clever if cynical approach: pump up the poor with a little boost of self-importance as they gulp down their alcohol on an empty stomach.

On the road to Bassin-Bleu

We hurry our rest stop, as it's already midafternoon. A longer road awaits us, which, according to both Pablo and Leonardo, is even worse than the one we were on, unpaved and washed out in places. And now that Pablo has joined us, we have the numbers problem I never did figure out in my sleepless travels. How are we going to get six people inside the cab?

Someone will have to ride in back on the flatbed. Leonardo out-and-out refuses, upsetting Bill, who's already frustrated with our useless guide. But I can understand how the young man feels: after a two-year absence, he wants to arrive home in style, not coated in white dust from the unpaved road.

The gallant Pablo offers to ride in back. (No wonder the ladies fall for him!) But the road sends up such a dense cloud that we can't even see Pablo through the back window. We stop. We're not letting Pablo, or anybody, for that matter, ride in back. They'll be asphyxiated, not just coated with white dust.

"This is the way to become a white man in Haiti," Pablo jokes.

Somehow we pack four of us in that backseat, stopping only once at a roadside display where over a dozen women are selling mangoes. Each one has laid out her wares, basins and buckets overflowing with every conceivable size and color of mango, from a deep orange the size of a baseball to a yellow-green the shape of a sweet potato. Since we haven't met many vehicles on the road, where are these women planning to find customers?

It must be their lucky day, because soon after we stop, a truck pulls over, loaded with cane chairs and women sitting on sacks of charcoal. It turns out they aren't stopping to buy mangoes but to check us out.

The driver climbs down from his cab, taking this opportunity for a pit stop right on the road. But no one is looking at him. They're all intrigued with us, and as the only woman, with me. Comments and calls waft down.

In response, I reach my hands to them, and then, punch-silly from the terrible road, I call up, "Oh angels from on high, send your blessings down on me!" Pablo translates. The women must think this is hilarious, because they burst into laughter. Maybe there's a future for me as a stand-up comic in Haiti?

The stop lightens our spirits. There is something blessed about connecting with people so seemingly different with something as simple as laughter, though I suppose it would also work with tears.

From Pablo, who has been in most recent contact, we find out that we will actually be meeting up with Piti in Bassin-Bleu, an hour south of Port-de-Paix. Piti's family lives up in the mountains, west of the city, but Pablo believes the wedding will be taking place in a church right in town. It makes sense for us to stay in a hotel in Bassin-Bleu and not head out to the countryside tonight to be introduced to Piti's family, whom we will meet tomorrow at the wedding anyway. After nine hours on the road, it feels good to anticipate our arrival.

Bassin-Bleu, Bassin-Bleu, Bassin-Bleu, the alliterative name becomes my mantra. The promise of a bath, supper, a night of rest . . . A Graham Greene scene begins playing in my head — the handicap of readers whose first experience of a place is often in print: expats with a past, beautiful women, a terrace, palm trees swaying under the stars, soft lights at the bar, drinks with little umbrellas, hip-swaying music. What will I order for dinner?

But after a couple of hours, the hot, gritty reality breaks in. Spirits flag. We are weary, we are hungry, cramped and cranky inside the cab. The going is rough: washed-out roads, impromptu detours through dried riverbeds. Suddenly I start wondering what would happen if it should rain? What if the rivers flood? We've taken the precaution of bringing a tarp to protect our luggage, but what about our lives? More immediately, what if the pickup breaks down?

Almost as if in answer, we come upon a stand, a shredded tarp thrown over four poles. Nailed to the poles are horizontal bars draped with every conceivable automotive part you can think of.

It looks like a vehicle has been disemboweled and its entrails are on display. Hanging from a nearby branch, a sign reads:

JEAN JONAS AUTOPARTS
PIECES POUR: TOYOTA-ISUZU
GROS CAMION-MOTO-BICYCLETTE

That about covers everything we've seen on this road. No sign, however, of Jean Jonas, though across the way, there is a church made of small river stones. It must have taken forever to build, but at least the materials were portable. The church is locked up, not a soul in sight. But perhaps Jean Jonas is inside praying for a customer as we ride by.

Arrival at Bassin-Bleu

For the dangling carrot at the end of a nine-hour stick of bad roads, Bassin-Bleu turns out to be a disappointment. This is not the Bassin-Bleu you will get among the top hits if you Google *Bassin-Bleu, Haiti*. Instead, you'll be directed to the beautiful waterfalls, also known as Bassin-Bleu, frequented by visitors in the hills west of Jacmel in the lusher, more prosperous south. This Bassin-Bleu is a dry, dusty city of empty streets and deserted-looking wooden houses. The few concrete residences have iron grilles in front, the doors locked, the windows closed, the shutters shut.

We park on the main thoroughfare, looking around for Piti. It occurs to me: where exactly in this city of thirty thousand are we to meet him? "Meet you in Bassin-Bleu" is not exactly like saying, "Meet you in the only gas station on the road between Limbé and Ennery."

But by now, I've surrendered to the rhythms of this

adventure, albeit with periodic attacks of anxiety, when the road washes out or the possibility of flash floods or other misadventures occur to me. I'm trusting in angels from on high to shed their blessings down on all of us. And this approach seems to be working: Pablo and Leonardo go in one of the houses and return with good news. They've called Piti, who is setting out right now from the country-side and should be here very soon. "Very soon" turns out to be another of those flexible terms, like "almost there." We will wait for over an hour before Piti arrives.

"It seems the wedding will not be in Bassin-Bleu," Pablo adds, as if this is an insignificant detail.

My heart sinks. Have we come so far for nothing? "So where is the wedding going to be?"

"Where the bride lives."

"Where is that?"

"Just beyond where Piti's family lives."

I decide not to ask how far that is.

What's surprising is that Pablo has found out this information, not from Piti himself, but from the inhabit-ants of the house where he made the phone call. Accord-ing to them, there are no weddings scheduled in any of the Bassin-Bleu churches tomorrow.

How do they know? The city is sizable enough to merit its name on maps. But this is not the first time I've been astonished by the capacity of oral cultures in our so-called underdeveloped little countries to get the news out. By now, all of Bassin-Bleu must know about the arrival of three whites, one brown Dominican, and two Haitians, looking for a wedding that will not be taking place in any Bassin-Bleu church tomorrow.

In front of where we are parked, a couple of girls sit on a concrete stoop leading up to one of the locked houses. They watch us with sidelong glances, but continue with their work: one is braiding the other's hair.

A young man in a sky-blue shirt with a Lacoste logo and a notebook approaches us. He looks professional, perhaps because of the notebook, the logo shirt, the folded arms of someone sizing us up. He knows a little English. "Hello, my friend, can I help you?" he asks me.

I smile, uneasily. Something about him reminds me of pushy salesladies following me around in a store. "No thank you. We are just waiting for a friend."

The girl who was having her hair combed joins him, her front braiding still unfinished, so she has a wild Afro on the aft part of her head like the mane of a lion. As the pair examines me, their glances change from curiosity to a look of blatant appraisal that disappears me and sees only what of value I am wearing.

The girl starts in, pointing to a little medallion on a gold chain around my neck, and then to herself. I shake my head. Although she can't understand me, I explain that it's my Virgencita. She protects me. The girl points to my left hand. How about the rings? I explain: this is my wedding ring, this is my engagement ring. On my right hand are my high school graduation ring and a garnet ring that belonged to Bill's mother. Suddenly, I see myself through this girl's eyes: a white woman wearing a watch, a medallion, earrings, and *four* rings. I am a rich woman in Haiti and flaunting it.

"I am hungry," the young man takes up the petitioning. "Give me something." The plea becomes more and more insistent. The girl joins in. If the roadside encounter with the truckload of women early this afternoon was a moment of grace, all differences obliterated as we joined in laughter, this encounter is its opposite. A gulf has opened between us, one that cannot be bridged by humor or friendship or courtesy. I turn away, reduced to my possessions, feeling the insult of my presence in this place.

Meeting no success with me, they turn to the men in my party. The young woman asks the man in the blue shirt to translate a phrase for her. "Come to me," she repeats, addressing Homero, who grins and shrugs. She gets the same response from Eli and Bill. Leonardo and Pablo have been hanging back, not fully understanding that this is not a friendly encounter. But now they come forward and extricate us.

Accommodations?

While we are waiting for Piti, we decide to check out the hotels. We ride down to the corner gas station, and a discussion ensues in Kreyòl. We finally get the translation: it turns out there are only two hotels in Bassin-Bleu, and one is not completed; in fact, construction stopped a while ago. The other hotel is a deserted-looking building beside the gas station with a dangling sign in front that reads HOTEL & RESTAURANT. The door is locked. We peer through the dirty windows at the abandoned lobby. No trace of a restaurant within. The word goes out to the owner that he might have some customers.

A large man appears in a ripped T-shirt and cutoffs, a bandana around his head. He has the build of a football player and an impressive keychain, which marks him as an important man around town. Someone who owns things that have to be kept under lock and key. It takes him a while to locate the key that will open the hotel door. Not a good sign. When was the last time there was a guest in this town? It turns out that the restaurant is not presently operating, but the owner can provide a meal if we'd like one. As for water and electricity, unfortunately, the generator for the city has been broken for months.

We pick our way through the trash heaped in the hallways inside. Even in the waning light, the tour confirms our suspicion: every room is filthy, the beds unmade, a coating of dust everywhere. The closed-up rooms are like saunas without air conditioning, ventilation, or fans.

But even if we decide to stay here—because what other options are there?—where would we put our vehicle overnight? The hotel has no secure parking area. "I'm not leaving the pickup out here," Bill declares, shaking his head at me as if I've suggested any such thing. I can guess what he's thinking. If he leaves the pickup on the street, by tomorrow its disassembled parts will be part of Jean Jonas's inventory.

As we are conferring outside about what to do, Piti appears, walking briskly down the road that leads into town, flanked by two young men who turn out to be his brothers, Jimmy and Willy. They might as well be angels coming from on high, we are so pleased to see them. Piti rushes toward us, his arms spread in welcome, his face radiant. We hug him, we hug his brothers.

"Little Piti is getting married!" we half-tease, half-congratulate him. He grins from ear to ear, and the years fall away. For the moment, the problem with accommodations is forgotten.

When he hears our predicament, Piti explains that his family will put us up. All along, this has been his plan. As for a meal, there is also food. "But we are poor," Piti adds apologetically. "There is not much food. But there is food." We decide to visit a supermarket before we leave town and buy some supplies to contribute to the meal. This turns out to be harder than we think. There seems to be no supermarket in Bassin-Bleu, and the market is not opened at this hour. But an onlooker points to the station. There is a minimarket inside. We walk over to check it out.

It is interesting to consider what consumer food products have found their way to this remote corner of Haiti: ten bottles of Del Monte ketchup, half a dozen big boxes of cornflakes, four cans of Pringles, some cartons of fruit juices, five jars of mayonnaise, a stack of evaporated milk cans, and some jars with red lids whose beige contents might be peanut butter. There is also a whole top shelf of wine bottles and hard liquor. In short, nothing to make a supper out of, although we could just clean out the alcohol and the chips and make a wedding rehearsal bash out of it! But that wouldn't work. As devout evangelicals, Piti and his family will not touch alcohol.

The proprietor, who has been out at the pumps filling up motorcycles with small amounts of gas, comes in to find out what he can sell us. We shake our heads bashfully. We are not proving to be very good patrons of what Bassin-Bleu has to offer.

As we come out of the gas station store, I spot a truck parked across the street. Scrawled on the dusty cab in red graffiti, this message:

> LIKA OBAMA
> VOTE # I

I recall the day in January when our new president was inaugurated. I happened to be visiting my parents in Santiago, and after watching the ceremony on cable TV, I ran down to the grocery store, still wearing my *Sí Se Puede* Obama T-shirt. Boys stocking shelves and cashiers ringing up purchases came forward to high-five me. Eight months later, reading Obama's name on the side of a dirty truck in this desolate spot in Haiti, I feel a kindred surge of hope. Here, too, people are waiting for their miracle to happen.

To Moustique, Charlie's house, a big-hearted welcome

It's close to dark and we still have a ways to go. "The roads are very bad," Piti says, apologetically, as if he were responsible.

How bad can a bad road get to best the worst we have already traveled? We soon find out. So far, we have at least been on discernible roads, and the rivers we've forded have been dry. But now we must cross Trois Rivières. From my long forgotten but suddenly resuscitating high school French I recall that *trois* means three. We will have to ford a river that's a confluence of three?

Deftly, Piti navigates us over the shallow spots. *(Over to the left! Straight ahead! No, no, no, over to the right some more!)* The rest of us in the cab echo his instructions, as if our beleaguered driver, Bill, can't comprehend Piti's injunctions but needs a Greek chorus to enlighten him.

Once on the other side, we drive along a path the pickup helps widen. We are headed for Moustique, Piti explains, the name of the countryside where his family and his bride live. "Moustique, moustique." Homero keeps repeating the word. He is almost sure *moustique* is the Kreyòl word for mosquito. Bill and I glance at each other, recalling a discussion in Vermont about whether to bring mosquito nets on our trip. Thank goodness we agreed it was a sensible measure given the widespread occurrence of malaria in rural Haiti.

Forty minutes later, we arrive at the house where we will be staying. To think that Piti and his brothers actually walked this distance earlier this afternoon! No wonder we waited over an hour for them to come. Now I know why they were mopping their foreheads and necks with facecloths as they entered Bassin-Bleu.

The house where we will spend the night belongs to Charlie, whose sister is married to Piti's brother Jimmy, whom we just met. Piti's own house is farther in, not accessible by road, so this is a more convenient spot for us to spend the night. It's unclear if these arrangements were made beforehand or on the spot, as Piti disembarks first and pulls Charlie to one side. No matter. Charlie welcomes us as if his whole extended family has been preparing for days for our arrival.

Perhaps Charlie's sense of hospitality comes from having worked several years in a resort in the Bahamas. That's where he picked up a little English, heavily accented and disconcertingly British. The family seems relatively well-off. Though the house is small, four rooms, it is made of concrete with a zinc roof, in contrast to the mud-and-wattle constructions with thatched roofs we've seen along the way, which I actually find more beautiful.

Each room has a bed, the front room also accommodating a table with a paisley tablecloth, several chairs, and two cabinets with glasses and dishes. But where will they all sleep if we take the three beds they are offering us? I've counted four grown sisters, two with husbands (one of these being Piti's brother Jimmy); two little girls and a toddler; as well as an old man with startling blue eyes whom Charlie introduces sweetly as "my daddy."

"There is plenty of room," Charlie assures us. I don't

inquire further, assuming the family will redistribute it-self in surrounding houses. But when we wake up the next morning and go outside, we find everyone has slept on mats spread out under the trees. It's not lost on any of us: the generosity of those who are willing to share the little they have. It goes through my mind again, the scene with the girl and the young man in Bassin-Bleu.

Before we settle in, Leonardo needs a ride home. Bill, cranky after a twelve-hour drive, shakes his head, no. It's not far, Leonardo argues, which argument is used against him. If it's not far, he can walk.

"Come on, honey," I intervene.

Come on, honey, nothing. Leonardo has been totally useless as a guide. What's more, he's now doubling his charge — an extra hundred dollars, *and* he wants door-to-door service.

One of our vaudeville acts ensues. The boy hasn't seen his family in two years, I point out. ("He's not a boy!") He's too tired to walk. ("So am I, and I'm the one who's been driving all day!") So, I'll drive him. ("It's not that far.") Even if it's not far, Leonardo has to carry a suitcase and a box full of spaghetti *for his mother.* This poignant detail doesn't seem to affect Bill the way it does me. But then, the plight of small farmers doesn't make me want to join their struggle by buying a coffee farm. The Leonardo impasse finally ends with a settlement: I'll stay with Bill, unpacking our things, and Homero and Eli will drive Leonardo home in the pickup.

It's a moment in the trip I will hate missing. Leonardo running out of the pickup, surprising his auntie sitting outside their front door. Homero recounts the cries of joy, the tearful embraces, the exclamations over the box of spaghetti. Bill listens, penitent, if defensive. "He might be poor, but he's still a spoiled brat." It may be, but even if it is spoiling, certain things—not counting my jewelry— seem a shame to withhold.

While Homero and Eli are off delivering Leonardo, our host Charlie shows us around. The outhouse is down a path, bordered by small bushes to which half a dozen scrawny goats are tied. Every time you head for the facilities, you set off a round of bleating, so everyone is apprised of all your movements, including the ones your bowels make. The bathroom is literally a place to bathe, a structure with a thatched roof and four sides covered in tarp. You lift a flap and enter. Inside there is a big basin and a small container for throwing water over yourself. As for the water itself, Charlie holds up a hand. "It is coming."

A little while later a sister and the two young nieces appear, carrying buckets from the river, which we know from having forded it earlier is a distance away.

The other hut behind the house is the kitchen, a small dark room, blackened from the charcoal fires inside. Above the door on a wooden plank someone has written a series of numbers. It turns out to be the cell phone of a fifth sister who is working in Florida, the mother of the two girls. I ask for their names.

Soliana shyly whispers hers. "Rica," the older, bolder one pipes up. She has a megawatt smile that makes you smile just to look at her.

"*Rica* means 'rich' in Spanish," I tell her. When Piti translates, Rica keeps smiling the same blinding smile as if this is no news to her. It occurs to me that with a number of uncles working in Spanish-speaking Dominican Republic, her lucky name was picked for a reason.

Tomorrow's plans, to bed at last

Night has fallen, and Piti and his brother Willy are due home. They will take shortcut paths where the pickup cannot go. It is a dark, moonless night, but Piti claims he could find his way blindfolded, as he has been walking these hills since he was a boy.

Before he leaves, we discuss plans for tomorrow. The wedding is supposed to take place at the unlikely hour of eight thirty in the morning. But this is actually a good thing, as our party will have to leave right after the ceremony. Tomorrow is Thursday. Unless we get to Cap-Haïtien tomorrow night, nine hours from where the wedding will take place, we will have a hard time making it to the border in one day before the gates close on Friday at five o'clock.

"We are coming with you," Piti decides on the spot. By we, he means his bride, Eseline, and their four-month-old baby girl.

"Piti, it's your wedding!" I try to reason with him. "Don't you want to stay and be with your family and other guests?"

Piti shakes his head. "There is the problem with money. I have used all the money."

Bill and I have already sent Piti some money for his

wedding present, but now we offer him some additional funds so he can stay for a few more weeks. Afterward, he can return with his family by bus or however it is one gets to the border from here.

But that is the problem, Piti explains. Why, he wants to go with us. The journey is long and rough. The ride in the air-conditioned cab of our pickup, even though crowded, will be so much easier on the young baby and on Eseline, who has never traveled far in a vehicle.

Later, of course, we will understand why Piti was so insistent on going with us. Years ago, we helped him acquire his passport, so he can travel easily back and forth. All he has to do is purchase a visa. But Eseline is another story. She has no passport, and since the marriage license won't be issued until two weeks after the wedding, no proof that she is married to Piti. But Bill and I are Americans, people of means. We will figure out a way to cross his family. Piti does not say any of this to us now. In fact, when I question him about documents for his wife and child, he assures me that all these arrangements can be made at the border.

I decide to follow the then current policy of the US military toward gays: *Don't ask. Don't tell.* Piti has made these crossings multiple times. He must know this plan can work; surely he wouldn't be exposing his young wife and child to danger and trauma. The less I know about these transactions, the better off we all will be, since, as people have often told me — starting with my mother, when I was a naughty child and would try to lie my way out of a punishment — my face betrays me.

But what about Eseline? "Shouldn't you talk this over with her first?" I say, sticking up for the female's right to decide.

"Tomorrow she is my wife and must do what I say," Piti explains, matter-of-factly.

"Piti!" How could the sweet boy I fell in love with years ago utter such a sexist comment? "You must talk it over with Eseline," I insist. Piti gives me a perfunctory yes-mom nod. I have a feeling the talk will not be the kind of conversation I am thinking of.

After we say our farewells, our group sits down at the table in the front room. No dinner seems forthcoming, so we unpack what's left of our snacks by the light of two candles. As we uncork the wine, our host appears bearing a pot of steaming rice, followed by Jimmy with a bowl of bean sauce, or so we think, though there's not a bean in sight. Charlie returns with a third pot of spicy goat's meat swimming in gravy, which Bill claims is the most delicious goat he has ever tasted.

I don't bother to ask how many times he has tasted

goat, but it's definitely not a staple of our Vermont diet, which tends to be primarily vegetarian in deference to me. I try a mouthful of the rice, avoiding the brown sauce, as I'm not sure what's in it. Dessert is some Hershey's Kisses that were lying around in our kitchen in Vermont since last Halloween. I was about to throw them out, but Bill intervened. "Save them for the trip. They might come in handy." Indeed, in this part of Haiti, where nothing is thrown away, they taste delicious. "The best stale Hershey's Kisses I've ever tasted," Bill jokes.

Soon after our meal, we brush our teeth under a spangle of stars and dive under our mosquito nets: Homero in one bed, Eli and Pablo in another, and Bill and I in the third one. The night is comfortably cool since we're up high above the dry basin where Bassin-Bleu lies. Remembering that hot, dirty hotel, I feel doubly grateful.

I fall asleep, wondering if Piti has made it home. What has Eseline said about their sudden departure tomorrow? According to Piti, Eseline has only traveled as far as Gros Morne, a little south of Bassin-Bleu. Again, from my high school French, I know *gros* means big, but I don't recognize *morne*. Maybe something to do with mourning? It is precisely what I imagine Eseline is feeling as she receives the news that tomorrow she and her baby will be borne away by a new husband, who doesn't even bother to discuss his plans with her beforehand.

August 20, a long wedding day & night

Preparations

I wake up to one of the pleasures I remember from childhood: sleeping under a mosquito net like a princess or some other precious being who needs to be veiled from the world.

For a while in my half sleep I've been hearing a rhythmic sound, not the patter of rain or anything mechanical. A human rhythm. I peek out the door and see one of Charlie's sisters sweeping the dirt yard with a broom made of straw. It hasn't rained in months; the ground is hard and dry, a grayish color. She sweeps away the fallen leaves, smoothes out any clumps. By the time she is finished, the yard is a tidy, uniform pale gray, except for one embarrassing darker spot where I, unwilling to walk all the way to the outhouse in the middle of the night, peed just outside the door. I recall a lecture given by Woody Tasch, author of *Slow Money*, in which he claimed that there are two kinds of people in this world: "those who shit in drinking water and those who don't." I've now added a third kind: people who pee in other people's front yard.

The rest of the family is still lying on mats under a tree in the backyard. Our own stirring wakes them, and preparations begin. The wedding will start at eight thirty, but since Bill and I are the official godparents, Piti wants us there at seven thirty. To get there, we will have to drive about twenty minutes, park the pickup on the side of the road, and hike in to the bride's family's house. Given those directions, I briefly consider wearing the same practical black jeans and I LOVE MY BARRIO T-shirt from yesterday, instead of the fancy outfit I packed when I thought this was going to be a church wedding—a long, flouncy, pale yellow skirt and jacket, a black camisole with lace edging, and impractical black sandals.

But Piti is getting married, and I'm going to his wedding in style! There is no mirror, but when I come out of the house all gussied up, I can see myself reflected in my hosts' eyes. I must look as strange as the proverbial British colonial in his starched white suit and safari hat sitting down to tea in the middle of the jungle.

Perhaps because there is no mirror—or none we can see—the men shave each other. Meanwhile, Piti's sister-in-law, Tanessa, irons her husband's white shirt on the bedding still lying under the shade tree. She uses a contraption

I've never seen before: a heavy, hinged iron with hot coals in the inside compartment. I'm as intrigued by her iron as she is by my outfit. When she offers to iron my wrinkly skirt, I shake my head. I'm going to a wedding in rural Haiti, after all, not to high tea in a British colony.

It's already seven fifteen! Quickly, our group grabs a breakfast of cereal and evaporated milk, along with some of the mangoes from yesterday's stop. We're ready to roll! But our hosts insist on serving us breakfast: the leftovers from last night — a pot of rice, a bowl of brown bean juice, a small bowl of goat's meat. Only Pablo seems to have enough appetite for a whole second breakfast.

On the drive over, Bill again notes how, unlike the Dominican countryside, we don't see any mounds of trash on the road. It seems nothing is thrown away here in Moustique. I recall seeing the lid of one of the evaporated milk cans I opened being used by the two young girls to cut off a piece of rope for washing the morning dishes. That cut piece was unraveled, the strands bunched together for a scrubber. Meanwhile, the rest of the rope was threaded through a hole in the door of the kitchen to serve as a handle.

We finally pull over under one of those precious commodities in Haiti, a tree with shade. The horrible erosion we've read about is borne out by the brown hillsides everywhere we turn. We can see why. Here and there, fires smolder, trees being burned for charcoal, which provides 80 percent of the energy used in the country. What else are the people to do? Truly one of those environmental and social-justice conundrums; what should come first: the eradication of poverty or the forestation of the land that might allow for agriculture so that hunger can begin to be eradicated? *I am hungry. Give me something.* The chant starts up in my head.

To Eseline's house we go

Now the fun part starts for the lady in the long, flouncy skirt and dressy sandals. She keeps tripping over the skirt; the sandals don't give her purchase on the steep, rocky hillsides that go down and up as if imitating a rollercoaster. My beloved, in a floppy hat to guard his fair complexion, is having his own difficulties negotiating the rough terrain.

Pablo comes to my rescue, offering me his arm. He looks dashingly handsome in the tan suit that was in the hanging bag yesterday. The two of us could be headed for a wedding in Cape Cod. It's amazing he doesn't trip, given the shoes he is wearing with long, pointy toes, a style which is all the rage in the DR. Eli and Homero are much more casually dressed in jeans and khaki pants respectively, both with white shirts, in deference to the wedding, I suppose. Charlie has donned a striped shirt with a crest of a lion rampant above his right breast, very British, maybe from his time in the Bahamas. Bringing up the rear is a young Haitian man on a mule, dressed in a pale yellow suit, the same color as my skirt. "He, too, works in la République," Pablo points out. How can he tell? Anyone who can afford a suit has gotten out.

The hike is long and strenuous. Finally, after forty-five minutes, we descend into a clearing with half a dozen small houses arrayed around each other. The most prominent turns out to be Eseline's house, its mud walls a pale cream, the blue windows outlined in orange, the thatched roof peaked like the curl on top of a baby's head. A long awning of palm branches extends from the front door. It looks like an impromptu structure, perhaps put up for the wedding, so guests don't have to stand in the hot sun.

The cry goes out that we have arrived. Men and women stop what they are doing — carrying firewood, making fires, cooking, ironing, braiding hair, sweeping, preparing coffee — to look at us. A pack of children, always the best alarm, like geese in a barnyard, race down the side hills but brake to a stop ahead of us. It's as if *we* are the wedding party.

Piti comes bounding out from the back of Eseline's house in a white T-shirt to greet us. It's already eight thirty, and he is not even dressed. The wedding is obviously delayed, though Piti assures us that as soon as the pastors arrive, it will begin. There is no sign of the bride's family, and Eseline herself is off at a neighbor's house being dressed.

Piti calls a diminutive older couple to come forward. His mother and father, he says, introducing them to us. I embrace the thin, kerchiefed woman, whom I've been imagining for years praying for her son in a far-off land.

From the introductions that follow, I know that Piti's father has at least one other wife present, though I don't know if this is a subsequent wife, an ex-wife, or both wives are current. There are many sisters and brothers, half brothers and sisters. It's difficult to keep everyone straight, especially when we don't speak Kreyòl.

Piti disappears to get dressed, and Pablo and Charlie wander off to visit with friends. Eli and Homero and Bill and I are left with the rest of the mostly female guests, none of whom speaks Spanish or English. We glance around, not wanting to be too obtrusive, though, of course, that's impossible. Every person with whom we make eye contact offers us his or her seat, cleaning off the spots they have vacated with facecloths, which seem to be what is used here for handkerchiefs. I respond to every look or nod with a smile like a dignitary's wife at a function, whose only role is to look friendly.

Several of the children are openly curious, pointing to one or another of us: Bill with his silly hat, Eli with his red hair, me with the fancy outfit and impractical sandals. One little boy stares with big, astonished eyes. When I approach him, using my rudimentary French, to pronounce myself *votre amie* ("your friend" — at least I think that's what I said), he bursts into tears and runs to the safety of his mother's lap. "He's probably never seen a white person before," Bill guesses.

I'm intrigued by the motley dress of the gathering, which actually seems right in keeping with our own group's varied wear. Many of the women are in house-dresses; some in what look like summer nightgowns. One of Piti's sisters wears a flashy shirt blazoned with a huge motorcycle and a straw hat with four plastic leaves pinned in front. Another woman has on a bright pink dress and a tiny evening purse of faux leopard skin. The female dress code seems to be to wear the best you've got, including some favorite accessory: a straw hat, a handbag, a beaded neck-lace. In contrast, most of the men are casually dressed in T-shirts, pants, and cutoffs, except for the two suits, status symbols for sure.

While we, the women, and some older men sit, wait-ing, many of the young men crowd around a card table placed smack in the center of the path to the house. A domino game has been going on since we arrived. The players, who are sitting down, rotate with those standing, with no break in the playing. In fact, the game will continue throughout the wedding, the only concession being that the table will be moved out of the way to a shady spot under a mango tree.

Eseline's house seems to be the center hub, with paths like spokes leading off to other family houses. Down one of those paths, a woman approaches, bearing a small table on her head. The sunken top of the table is actually a canister with refreshments, which I assume will be served at the wedding. But, in fact, this turns out to be the cash bar: warm sodas, two boxes of cigarettes, penny candy, and a large jug filled with a drink no one buys, perhaps a home brew for nonevangelicals.

JULIA ALVAREZ

As for complimentary wedding refreshments, a woman comes out of Eseline's house with a laundry basket full of chunks of bread, which she forks out to anyone who approaches. Her red T-shirt reads ANGEL, a halo above and a wing on either end of the word. Another woman in a housedress with a kerchief tied around her head pours coffee from a white kettle, then washes the used and soon-to-be-recycled cups in a plastic basin. Mostly men and elderly women avail themselves of their services. The few young women who approach do so shyly, murmuring apologetically as if embarrassed to be enjoying other women's hard work when they themselves are fit, able, and female.

Meanwhile Piti's plump baby is brought out for us to meet. Loude Sendjika, I'm told, when I ask for her name. Perhaps affected by the same terror of white skin as the little boy, she starts bawling the minute she is laid in my arms. It could also be that I'm holding her in the nursing position but have nothing to offer her. A young woman lifts her from my arms and starts nursing her. Throughout the long wait and ensuing ceremony, Loude Sendjika is handed around to whatever lactating female is close by, a great way for moms to help out the indisposed bride.

Where is the pastor?

It's already after nine, and the pastor has still not arrived. Piti comes from the back of the house to check on us. The worried look in his eyes has intensified. We learn why the wedding wasn't in Bassin-Bleu. The pastor refused to marry the couple inside a church, because, with a four-month-old, Piti and his girlfriend had obviously had relations. Instead he consented to perform the ceremony at the bride's house. But maybe he has changed his mind?

Another person who has not shown is Leonardo. I worry that he decided to stay away after his altercation with Bill last night. More likely, he's making the most of his short visit. Homero mentioned an attractive young woman, joining the joyous reunion last night, a little boy and girl at her side. Maybe Leonardo is married, the spaghetti to be shared between wife and mother? At any rate, he will be returning to the Dominican Republic after a couple of weeks, using the smuggler's route — the reason he might have needed the extra cash.

We've about given up wishing the pastor would get here. But then, like the old fairy-tale warning, *Be careful what you wish for,* here come not one, but two, then three, and finally four more, seven pastors in all, dressed in black suits, white shirts and black ties, bearing Bibles. It turns out that only one is the pastor, the others are "predicators," members who preach and sing and share pastoral responsibilities. Accompanying them is one woman, dressed similarly in a white blouse and black skirt, the pastor's wife. All I can think of as they each come down the path and enter the house, nodding their greetings left and right, is: This is going to be a *long* service, with lots of preachers wanting to put in their word on the word of God.

The wedding ceremony

Finally, with less fanfare than I expected, Piti is coming down the dirt path with his beautiful bride in full regalia: a full-length long-sleeved white gown with a long train and a bouquet of artificial flowers. Behind her is Pablo, the best man, and behind Piti is an attractive woman in her forties whom I at first assume is the bride's mother. But it turns out she is Eseline's baptismal godmother. Eseline's mother will not be attending the ceremony. She is too broken up about her daughter's imminent departure, so we are told.

We proceed inside the small house whose front room
has been emptied. A white sheet covers the dirt floor;
another is draped over the two chairs for the bride and
groom. Two other chairs have been set up behind these,
also covered with a white sheet, for Bill and me, the godparents of the wedding. I take a seat behind Piti, and Bill
behind Eseline, but the pastor summons Pablo to correct
the error: the godmother must sit behind the bride and the
godfather behind the groom. I'm a little surprised over the
exactitude of these ceremonial details in such a rough-and-
ready place.

The pastor, predicators, and closest family members find their seats on the benches and chairs lining the walls. Everyone else takes turns gawking through the four windows and doorway. Intermittently, the faces change. Someone else is given a turn to watch a part of the ceremony. The only problem is that such clustering at all apertures cuts off the ventilation and flow of air for the rest of us inside.

The ceremony starts unpleasantly with bride and groom being reprimanded for having had relations before marriage. They must endure public humiliation as each predicator opens his remarks with a finger-wagging, punitive tone that even I, with not a word of Kreyòl, can tell is a scold.

But finally, the tone shifts. The pastor, who looks like the oldest of these elders, keeps his rebuke brief. I wonder if it's the old good cop / bad cop routine, and before their arrival, the pastor told his predicators: "Give them hell! And leave the rest to me." He begins by calling out chapter and verse to one or another of his predicators, who finds the passage in his Bible and reads a sentence or two at a time. The pastor repeats the passage, then he's off, spinning stories, enacting examples, delivering cautions that often bring the house down. Every once in a while, a grinning Piti repeats a phrase to Eseline, wagging his finger at her. No doubt we're deep into St. Paul and his admonitions to wives to submit to their husbands, no questioning them when they say we are moving to la République in a couple of hours.

Loude Sendjika is present, happily sucking away at some young mother's breast. She is dressed in one of those overly frilly dresses that must be prickly and hot, and a knit cap that surely makes her even hotter. The outfit is a robin's-egg blue, which seems a favorite shade in this area of rural Haiti: the color of many doors and shutters, of shirts and skirts and blouses, and most pervasively of the clear, endless summer sky above, which hasn't sent down any rain in two months.

At some point between feedings, Loude Sendjika starts to fuss. I entertain the mischievous thought of handing her over to the bride to clap to her breast, in defiance of all the scolding predicators. But the bodice of Eseline's gown is a tight fit. And sitting behind her, I can see that she has been stitched inside a gown that is actually several sizes too big for her. It turns out to be a rental, the dress that all the young girls in the settlement have gotten married in. One size fits all, indeed.

The best part of the ceremony, especially for those of us who don't understand Kreyòl, is the singing. Since there are no hymnals, and most of the people gathered here could not read them anyway, one predicator or another calls out the words, and then the gathering sings them, phrase after phrase, beautiful harmonies, hypnotic repetitions, and cycling of voices. The choruses seem to go on forever, as if everyone is reluctant to leave the enchantment of the music.

The classic moments of weddings are here — the slipping on of rings, the exchange of vows — but with slight revisions: Piti slips a ring on Eseline's finger, but he does not get one. Later, Piti will explain that he could only afford one ring. At first, Eseline's family had insisted on earrings as well, and this actually became a deal breaker that delayed the wedding for months. Finally, her family relented. I'm left wondering if my petitioners in Bassin-Bleu were in a similar pickle and had to produce a piece of jewelry to some demanding relation.

As for the vows, instead of one summary vow, repeated by each partner, the pastor reads an endless list, after which each must repeat, *"Wi pastè"* ("Yes, pastor"). Piti's voice is confident and resounding, Eseline's barely a whisper. The ceremony finishes with both bride and groom kneeling on the sheet, embracing each other, while all the predicators stand and lift hands, calling down blessings on the new husband and his wife.

But the ceremony is not over yet. A bottle of champagne is brought out and placed on a small stool in the center of the room. I'm puzzled, since Piti's evangelical religion does not permit drinking. But again, the champagne turns out to be another import from traditional Western weddings: not quite a toast but a ceremonial drink to seal the marriage. As the godmother, I'm supposed to open the bottle, but I struggle without success.

Bill steps forward to help me, intending to give the cork a mere twist, so I can do the rest. But the minute he turns the cap, the cork pops out and a spume of champagne sprays half the room. Whatever that means in the iconography of wedding symbols (robust sex, many children, a fountainhead of blessings), the baptism of champagne brings on a burst of laughter. A tray of four glasses is held out to me: I pour the groom and his bride each a drink, and then two others, which turn out to be for us, the godparents. Bill and I take dainty sips, not sure if we're meant to pass our glasses around to the assembled party.

By now, we are sweating profusely, and although there have been resounding amens and a concluding hymn, no one makes a move to go outdoors. In fact, the bride's father stands, inspired, to address the new couple. He is a tall, thin man, dressed in what look to be his work clothes. Since Bill and I can't understand him anyway, we slip outside.

Later, Piti will tell us that Eseline's father was full of sincere congratulations. This was a big change. Earlier, his future father-in-law had been understandably dubious about this young man who had gotten his daughter pregnant. Who knew what Piti had been up to, so many years away in another country? All that time, making real money, and he couldn't buy his bride a set of earrings! But when the community learned that Piti's American friends and former employers were coming all the way across Haiti for his wedding, Piti's social capital shot up. His father-in-law now feels secure entrusting his eldest daughter into his hands. This alone is worth the trip to Piti's wedding.

How do you say good-bye in Kreyòl?

Soon after her father's address, the bride makes the rounds outside, kissing everyone, accepting their good wishes, and saying her good-byes.

Piti does not accompany her. No longer at the mercy of the pastor and predicators, he takes off to settle some last-minute business. He returns in street clothes, suitcases packed, ready to go. Eseline is hurried away by her god-mother to change. But before we depart, the families insist: we must eat.

We are ushered into the back room where a card table has been set up. Women run back and forth from the kitchen hut, carrying in plates and utensils (fork or spoon—choose, you can't have both). The food arrives piecemeal, as each dish is ready—for we are eating ahead of the guests. First comes a pot of rice with actual beans mixed in it, in honor of the occasion; a little later, some more bean sauce; then, the goat meat; finally, a bowl of steaming boiled plantains, as if someone over at the kitchen counted up all the dishes and thought: that's not enough.

Piti and Eseline, now in traveling clothes, are seated at the edge of the bed, the rest of us wedged in around the table. At first, Eseline just stares down at her plate, glum and disinterested. So many monumental events packed into one day! No doubt she has butterflies in her stomach. We all urge her to eat. There is a long road ahead. This wedding meal will have to serve us until we make Cap-Haïtien tonight. Later we will regret having encouraged her.

One traditional wedding moment Piti and Eseline will forego is the cutting and serving of the wedding cake, actually three cakes. They are stacked one above the other on a wooden stand that has been wrapped in aluminum foil to make it look festive. It seems there wasn't enough frosting to go around, because each cake has bare patches, discreetly turned toward the wall.

Before we leave, two of the cakes are wrapped up in the stand's foil: one for Piti to share with his bride, the other for Bill and me. This means the rest of the guests, about sixty people, are to share the remaining one, which just doesn't feel right. Deep down, I do believe, we all know it stinks: the injustice of how the world's goods are distributed. But this is one of those moments when I don't have to speak the language to know that it would be an insult for me to refuse our hosts' generosity.

Finally, we are good to go. How do you say good-bye in Kreyòl? *Orevwa*, I'm told. *Orevwa, orevwa,* I keep repeating, as I hug Piti's father, Eseline's father, and Charlie, who will be staying on to eat with the other guests. Piti's mother and I hold each other for a second longer than just saying our good-byes. How do you say: I have often thought of you? How do you say: I understand how hard it is to see them go? When we pull apart, both our eyes are moist. This is how you say those things that are hard to say in any language.

Bill and Eli and I take the lead up the hillside path. It is high noon. Stopping to rest on a hilltop, we can see the small house in the clearing, the guests gathering under the awning, beginning to be served their dinner.

Below us, coming up the path is the wedding party: close friends and family accompanying the couple to the road where the pickup is parked. Pablo is carrying the suitcase in which the couple's and the baby's belongings have been packed. Another friend carries the two cakes, the third the bottle of champagne. In a pink dress with matching headscarf comes Eseline with her baby under a matching pink parasol. Bringing up the rear is her favorite sister, Rozla, the one who follows her in the family of six girls, one son. She is wearing a salmon dress that matches Eseline's in every detail but color. The two sisters are the same build, the same height, similar features. In fact, an outsider who has yet to learn to look at people of a different race might mistake them for each other.

At the road, the sisters embrace. As Eseline climbs into the pickup, stony-faced, her sister collapses, weeping at the foot of a mango tree. They have no idea when they will see each other again. How will they survive this cruel separation? Two sisters who have spent their whole lives together, "two lovely berries molded on one stem, . . . two seeming bodies, but one heart," as Shakespeare describes that intense female bond in *A Midsummer Night's Dream*. It is not just marriage that can make one soul out of two separate beings.

Piti tries to comfort his new sister-in-law, then Pablo tries. There is no consoling her, so I don't know why I even try. I put my arms around her, and even though she can't understand my Spanish, I promise her that I will take care of her sister. No harm will come to her or to Loude Sendjika.

Tomorrow, when we arrive at the border, without a shred of evidence that these are Piti's wife and child, when we are frustrated with Piti for putting his young family and us in this predicament, when the most convenient thing would be to just give them some money and let them find their own way back to Moustique or across the river with untrustworthy smugglers at night, I will remember this promise to Eseline's sister. I will not abandon them. Not that I could have done otherwise, even had I not promised. There is a bottom line below which you cannot go and still call yourself a human being.

The long ride to Cap-Haïtien

It is way past noon by the time we're back at Charlie's house to collect our baggage, change into our travel clothes, and be on our way. About twenty minutes into the bumpy ride, that wedding meal we all urged Eseline to eat comes back to haunt us all.

We stop hurriedly for her to scramble out and vomit. I dig out some alcohol from my overnight case, dab her forehead, then hold the little bottle under her nose. Once she feels a little better, we climb back in the pickup. But this will keep happening throughout the eight-hour trip from Charlie's house to Cap-Haïtien, even when there can't possibly be any food left in her stomach. Piti reminds us that Eseline has only ridden in a vehicle a handful of times, and then only as far as Gros Morne, an hour south of Bassin-Bleu.

In her condition, she can't possibly handle a crying infant. Loude Sendjika is handed up front to me. Unfortunately, I can't do much to soothe the hungry baby. I think back on all those lactating mothers in Moustique. This is the first of many losses both Eseline and Loude Sendjika will feel keenly in the weeks and months to come. I, too, would be bawling if I were them.

Part of the baby's discomfort might well be the heat. She feels damp all over, and I've checked; it's not urine. I take off her knit cap, which her parents have insisted she wear, and unbutton her long-sleeved jumpsuit. Underneath, her little torso is tightly wrapped in a white cloth with safety pins in back. What on earth is this for? To keep her insides from getting jostled on the road, Piti explains. This is my first encounter with that Biblical article of wear, *swaddling clothes*, what Jesus was supposedly wrapped in when he was born and taken on a mad scramble out of Bethlehem by his terrified parents. Trotting on a donkey through a desert must be akin to riding in a pickup on the back roads of Haiti.

Bewildered as to what to do for the unhappy baby, I start singing her every lullaby sung to me as a child. A few incorporate the name of the baby being sung to. In order not to throw off the rhythm of the lyrics with the polysyllabic name, Loude Sendjika, I improvise the sobriquet, "Ludy," and it sticks. We all start calling her Ludy, including later Eseline and Piti. Ludy quiets down and smiles up at me, her round face so clearly Piti's.

Soon, her eyelids start to droop. Every time we go over a pothole or ford a river, I worry that she will wake up. But Ludy sleeps on. Her poor mother is not faring as well, gagging in the back seat. We can't keep stopping, or we will never make it to Cap-Haïtien before midnight. Instead, we rearrange ourselves, giving her one of the back windows, so she can hang her head out and vomit when she needs to. Pablo and Eli and Homero decide to ride in the flatbed, preferring the dust to the risk of being vomited upon. After a while, the weary Eseline lies down on her husband's lap and tries to sleep off her vertigo.

We stop at the gas station where we met up with Pablo and say our good-byes. From here Pablo will take a motorcycle-taxi to his front door, his hanging bag in one hand. He'll be wearing his beautiful suit again on Sunday, when he will make a formal proposal to his girlfriend's family for her hand in marriage. We've teased him that he will have to arrange for two marriages, one in Haiti, and one for his friends in the Dominican Republic. "We're getting too old to do this kind of trip again," Bill says half-jokingly.

We fill up with gas, and I encourage Eseline to take a walk around the station to try to shake off her dizziness. Piti remembers that there is a pill one can take. Of course:

Dramamine! I usually pack it in my overnight case, but I forgot to include it among my cautionary supplies. Maybe there is a drugstore nearby?

Piti inquires and is told that if we turn around and head away from our destination, toward Gonaïves, we'll run into a drugstore. But Bill vetoes the plan. It could be a saga of several hours trying to connect with Western medicine here in the middle of rural Haiti.

Night falls, arrival in Cap-Haïtien

Everyone is back inside the pickup: Homero in the co-pilot seat I've ceded to him, as he has done yeoman's service, riding in the flatbed for hours. Eseline, Piti, Eli, Ludy, and I are wedged in the backseat, alternating one forward, one back, to accommodate everyone. It's uncomfortable but a lot better than the public transport that Piti didn't want to subject his baby or wife to. We do have air-conditioning, and we are four instead of forty, packed in tight quarters.

As the shadows lengthen and night falls, the road grows pitch-black. This is precisely what we were trying to avoid by wanting to leave right after the wedding.

Piti remembers every major pothole, every washout, every impediment on the road and calmly alerts Bill to be on the lookout. I serve the opposite function, a kind of gasp-ometer, gasping every time we drop a foot into a pothole; or a fuel truck comes barreling around the bend, squeezing us off the road; or we swerve to avoid a washout and almost run over a child walking on the shoulder.

The road starts getting crowded — more and more buses, trucks, some cars; houses line either side. A sign with an arrow confirms that ahead lies Cap-Haïtien. By now, it is eight o'clock, totally dark, and I mean dark. This is not the urban night of a developed country with street lamps, neon signs, lit-up buildings that turn night into day. Except for a few pockets privileged with power, the road is dark, and the people are dark, and hard to spot walking on the shoulders. The gaspometer is stuck on gasp.

Finally, we arrive in Okap, as the Haitians have affec-tionately nicknamed their second-largest city. The streets are narrower, the houses closer, and there are more lights. What we are looking for is Hôtel Les Jardins de l'Océan, recommended by Madison, and located "in the Carenage just past the end of the Boulevard de Mer." Foolishly, we figure these directions are enough. After all, we met up with Pablo at "the gas station on the road to Ennery" and with Piti "in Bassin-Bleu."

But twenty minutes later, we are still twisting and turning in the boxlike grid of unmarked city streets. Where on earth is the Hôtel Les Jardins de l'Océan? The pedestrians we ask look thoughtful, as if pondering a philosophical question, finally shaking their heads. But at last, we find a young man who knows exactly where the hotel is and offers to ride with us so we don't get lost again.

Even without knowing the city, we can tell when we've reached the Boulevard de Mer, and not just because it runs by the sea. Hotels, awash in lights, flanked by waving palms, line the street. Not quite Graham Greene, but there is a different feel to this area. I'm reminded of that moment in *The Great Gatsby*, when Nick wonders out loud what is so very special about Daisy's low, thrilling voice, and Gatsby responds, "Her voice is full of money."

Okap has known the thrill of being "full of money." Back in the seventeenth and eighteenth centuries, Cap-Français, as it was known then, was the wealthy capital of the wealthiest colony in the world. But the city has also known its share of tragedies: having been destroyed three times by fire, in 1734, 1798, and 1802, then razed to the ground by an earthquake in 1842. *Sic transit gloria mundi.*

But tonight, exhausted and hungry, we're all ready for a little *gloria mundi.* According to Madison, the Hôtel Les Jardins de l'Océan is owned and run by a French woman, Myrième, and her chef son. "The restaurant is quite good," Madison mentioned in one e-mail. Back in Vermont, I didn't think much about this culinary tip. But now, it glows like the promise of paradise after a long stay in purgatory.

The hotel is not right on the boulevard but up a dark, twisting side street. We turn into a parking area at the base of a steep outdoor staircase leading up to the large house, built into the hill. One by one, we emerge from the pickup, a dirty, ragamuffin group. By the time we are all out of the cab, two porters have descended the steps to un-load our gear and show us where to park.

We ascend to the lobby, single file, like weary moun-tain climbers. Past the entryway, we find ourselves in a large room, the restaurant at the far end with a terrace view of the ocean. Sitting at a long table like a spider at the center of her web is a large white woman with cropped gray hair. Not much can escape her notice: traffic in any direction must go by her post: to the restaurant ahead, to the kitchen behind her, to a staircase on her left leading up to the guest rooms. On the table beside her are three cell phones, a calculator, a record book in which she has been finishing up the accounts for the day, and a fat glass of something that might be alcoholic. Madame Myrième, I presume.

Madame's sharp blue eyes look us over. Hoteliers must develop an instinct about who will or won't be trouble, especially in tricky, remote areas of the world. But Madame can't figure out our story and that has to be worrisome. Are we harmless missionaries? Aid workers? Are we running contraband? What is our connection to the young Haitians? The darling baby? Are Bill and I a childless couple looking to adopt the child? Is the young redheaded man our son? And if so, why would we want a baby? And who the hell is Homero?

The porters have finished bringing up our assortment of dusty luggage. It looks like we mean to move in for a while: three suitcases, several backpacks, a large cooler, an enormous cardboard box with our mosquito nets and other supplies spilling out of the top, two wedding cakes, an opened bottle of cheap champagne, and a plastic bag with a dirty diaper that has been doubling as Eseline's barf bag. Is there a trashcan where we can throw it out?

But the unforgivable affront to this French woman is that I should speak to her in English. Does she have any vacancies? She does not speak *anglais*, she tells me in *français*, shaking her head emphatically. So I switch to Spanish. Another adamant head shake. No Spanish either. "*Votre ami*, Madison Smartt Bell," I say in desperation, playing my last card. Again Madame Myrième shakes her head. She does not know anyone by that name.

Once again, Homero comes to the rescue. Some years ago, he was sent to France on a three month coffee-analysis course. Although it's now a little rusty, he used to be fluent in French. He pronounces Madison's name so it sounds French. Madame's face opens up. She repeats Madison's name so it sounds even more French. Of course, she has rooms for us.

Madame directs one of the porters to show us what's available for our approval. Is she kidding? Clean rooms with bathrooms and hot water, electricity, a ceiling fan, an air conditioner, cable television, and a French chef down in the dining room. Of course, we'll take them! Bill hands over his VISA — Madame will accept credit cards from the English-speaking world: eighty-five dollars per room, continental breakfast included. We follow our porter with his fistful of keys, each one attached to a wooden bar with the room number carved in it. On the second landing, Bill and I pick two side-by-side rooms, so that Piti and Eseline can be next door. We'll be able to help with the baby as well as with any instructions on using the facilities in their room. Given the way they've been glancing around, big-eyed, I have a feeling that neither has ever worked the buttons on an air conditioner or cruised the channels on a cable television with a remote control.

We agree to all meet down at the restaurant ASAP, as the porter has informed us that it closes at nine, fifteen minutes from now. Bill quickly showers and heads downstairs to the restaurant. I've told him to order for me. I really don't care what it is, as long as it's vegetarian and preceded by a glass of wine. A tall glass of white wine. As I'm undressing, I realize what I've been smelling on my clothes: champagne from the baptism Bill gave the whole congregation in trying to uncork the bottle. Another reason Madame might have been looking askance at me: I reeked of alcohol.

Once I've turned the shower off, I hear the baby crying next door. Poor Eseline, I think, needing to relax and recuperate. The crying goes on and on, finally turning that corner from the wailing of hunger to the shrieks of rage. I dress and hurry over — the door is unlocked — to find the baby on top of the bed all alone. Just then, Piti comes running into the room. It turns out that down on the main floor, Madame heard the baby crying — I said she didn't miss anything—and went over to the dining area to inform the parents.

"Piti, you left the baby alone?" I'm ready to give him a parental lecture, but I look at his round, worried face and think, Give the poor guy a break. He has already had a hard day, including scoldings from six predicators and a pastor. Besides, he is a new father, having just met his baby daughter a couple of weeks ago. What does he know about raising kids? Even Eseline, who has a four-month lead on child-rearing, thought it was okay to leave Loude Sendjika alone, with no pillows barricading her in the center of the bed and with the door closed, so they couldn't even hear her crying.

Piti and I go down to the restaurant together, the baby in my arms. Madame looks up, and I can see it in her eyes: she still hasn't figured out our story. But then, I haven't figured out hers either. How did a middle-aged French woman end up in Cap-Haïtien with her son, the chef?

For now, she has closed the record book and has a fresh drink before her. Maybe she has had a long day herself.

"*Bonsoir*, Madame," I say. She nods in reply as I pass by.

Why wine was invented

Everyone in our party is already seated at the table and served with drinks, tinkling with ice. I find my spot beside Eseline, who seems baffled by the amount of dinnerware and silverware before her. She follows my lead in everything but ordering. She's no vegetarian, and she must be starving. Homero translates the menu for all of us. The dishes sound very French: lamb with prunes on a bed of couscous; rabbit in a burgundy sauce; grouper with a puree of potatoes and a garnish of mango; a crepe topped with vegetables sautéed in butter, the sole vegetarian option.

Piti orders the goat and looks over at Eseline, no doubt thinking she will follow suit. But Eseline insists on the grouper, a surprising choice, given that grouper is a saltwater fish, and she has lived all her life in a landlocked area of rural Haiti. Even Piti questions her. Is she sure she wants the fish? Eseline nods, without hesitation. Maybe, she once ate fish when she visited Gros Morne, or she has heard of it and would like to taste it. A food associated with travel, excitement, a world beyond her life in Moustique. I recall arriving in New York City as a ten-year-old and feeling that way about grilled-cheese sandwiches and apple pie à la mode. This is what TV families ate. My husband would say that, as a vegetarian, my culinary tastes have not advanced much since then.

Part of my frustration with not speaking Kreyòl is that I can't talk with Eseline about all that is happening to her. (Just as I'll never know Madame's story for lack of French.) What does Eseline think of this place? Why did she order the grouper? What is she feeling? She has been stony-faced all day, uttering only a handful of words, mostly in a whisper, directed solely at Piti. More troubling, she seems disinterested in her beautiful baby. Recalling the parting scene with her sister and the long carsick ride, I imagine Eseline is still in shock. So many drastic changes have come her way in the last twenty-four hours.

But she perks up when the fish arrives. A quick study, she easily negotiates both fork and knife, eating up the uncharacteristically (for French cuisine) large portions on her plate. The table falls silent, everyone busily, happily eating away. Periodically, Bill and Homero break the silence, exclaiming over their wonderful dishes.

After finishing our main course, Eseline and I forego dessert and head upstairs, leaving the men behind. Our eyelids have been drooping, and Ludy is fast asleep in my arms. Outside her door, I wait for Eseline to unlock it before I hand her the baby. But instead, she takes her baby and hands me the keys. Suddenly, it strikes me: Eseline probably has never had to unlock a door before. Once she is safe inside her room, I go next door to mine and after a quick brush of the teeth and splash of water on my face, I hit the bed. I fall asleep instantly — that deep, profound sleep of childhood, before the worries set in, when you waded into bed and soon were in over your head.

Some time later (an hour, fifteen minutes?), I hear Bill enter the room, or at least I think it's Bill. (I once read an unbelievable tabloid story about a woman who sued a man for making love to her "under the pretense of being her husband." He had stolen into her bed one night as she slept so soundly that she claimed she could not tell the difference. After this night in Haiti, I can believe this woman's story.) So deep and restful is my sleep that I forget about tomorrow's border crossing, the mosquito bites that might bring on malaria, the coffee we drank that was made with water that might not have been brought to a boil or boiled long enough.

In my humble, culinarily compromised estimation, this soporific, lightening-of-the-load effect is why wine was invented. I can just imagine what Madame Myrième and her chef son would think of my opinion.

August 21, going home

Breakfast at Hôtel Les Jardins de L'Océan

I love waking up by the sea. The ocean is so much like the waters of sleep that the day ebbs into your dreams before your eyes are even open.

First, you smell it: a salty, nostril-flaring smell as if the earth itself is giving off perspiration. Then, you hear it: a lapping sound on the shore, the tinkling of rigging hitting against the masts of small boats. The sky outside the high window seems to have soaked up the ocean's deeper, dreamier blue.

Only one cloud stains the dreamy blue sky of my day: we will have to cross the border in a few hours, and no matter what Piti keeps saying, I don't think the guards will take our word that Eseline is his wife, and Ludy, his baby. And besides, wives and children still need their own documents. If it were not so, all poor men with visas to wealthier countries would be polygamists.

On the way down to breakfast, I stop to tell Piti and Eseline to meet us in the restaurant. They are sitting on the edge of their double bed, looking small and frightened, their suitcase packed at their feet, the baby in her arms. I wonder how long they have been waiting for one of us to come get them. There is a stuffy smell in the room. I look around. The windows are closed, and neither the overhead fan nor the air conditioner has been turned on. In the bathroom, the toilet has not been flushed. It's my fault. I was too tired last night to do for Eseline what Charlie did for us in Moustique: a crash course on using the amenities in the room.

Downstairs, Madame Myrième is already at her post, record book open, the three cell phones lined up next to the calculator. "*Bonjour*, Madame." This time I get a *bonjour* back.

Over toast and jam and eggs, and watery American coffee that has Bill shaking his head ("They should go to Moustique to learn to make coffee!"), we discuss the day's plans. We have to cross the border before it closes at five p.m., but maybe we should spend part of the day sightseeing? Once the colonial capital, Cap-Haïtien is steeped in history: the slave revolt that eventually freed the colony started in nearby Bois Caiman during a Vodou ceremony, so the legend goes. It'd be gratifying to tour the area with Piti and Eseline, who haven't seen much of their own country. And it is their honeymoon!

But talking it over with Homero, we change our minds. Today is Friday, market day at the border. Huge crowds move back and forth between the two countries, buying and selling everything from clothes to car parts to sacks of carbon to bottles of rum to cell phones to farm produce and animals. The bad side of all this commotion is that traffic virtually stops. Pickups, donkeys, wheelbarrows, carts, as well as men and women bearing loads, inch across the bridge. The good side is that during the height of this consumer chaos, the guards don't bother to check documents. But as closing time nears, security clamps down. Every vehicle, every pedestrian is scrutinized. It is best if we go in the middle of market day, and perhaps, *ojalá*, keep your fingers crossed, we will get across the border without being stopped.

Sounds like a no-brainer to me. Besides, how can any of us enjoy ourselves sightseeing while the worry hangs over our heads about what will happen at the border in a few hours? More and more, I am feeling caught in an old story, this time involving a Haitian, not a holy family, and on an island in the Caribbean, not a desert in Judea. But it makes sense that if a redeemer for the poor, the helpless, those at the margins were to come round again, he would choose the most impoverished country in the hemisphere to be born in.

A good cup of coffee, some Dramamine

Before we leave Okap, we decide to take a spin around town. *Spin* is actually not a word to use in connection with traffic in Cap-Haïtien. During the workday, it's difficult to move with ease: huge trucks stop two, three deep to unload their cargo; wares are laid out on sheets that extend into the street itself; pedestrians wind their way among stalled vehicles, pushing wheelbarrows or carrying loads on their backs. Brightly colored tap-taps, the little pickup trucks that serve as Haiti's main means of transport, display their curious names above their windshields in Kreyòl, French, English. How do the owners decide what to call them? I wonder. Some I can guess: PASSION, GOD BLESS, MERCI JÉSUS, TOUT EST POSSIBLE, but what about ILLUSION or MAMMA MIA or RABBI or KREYÒLA? And wouldn't an owner worry that he'd scare away potential passengers with a name like DEZESPERE, Despair?

I keep snapping pictures from the pickup. But every time I put down my window, a merchant approaches, even if I shake my head no, as if what I might not want from ten feet away will become irresistible when it's in my face.

Later I will e-mail Homero, asking him, as a Dominican, what most surprised him about Haiti. "The fact that, despite so much poverty, the lack of money, the bad economy, everywhere we went, people were selling something: whether it was mangoes on the road to Bassin-Bleu or car parts and pineapples in Cap-Haïtien or even the refreshments and cigarettes at the wedding. But who was buying?" In the case of the mangoes, I guess we were. But Homero is right: all along the streets of Okap, I don't see a single shopper, but almost everyone seems to want to sell us something.

What most surprised me? The white UN tanks that would come creeping eerily down the streets. True, I'd not been keeping up with Haitian news, but the only enemy I was seeing everywhere was poverty.

Maybe because a goal always helps to focus sightseeing, we decide to look for a drugstore to buy Eseline some Dramamine. Although the roads from here on out will be a lot better, it's still an hour to the border, and then a three-hour drive from Dajabón to my parents' house in Santiago, where we will spend the night. We want to spare her and ourselves a repeat of yesterday's saga. Bill also wants to find a café where he can drink a good cup of Haitian coffee before leaving the country.

But we might as well be the knights of the Round

Table searching for the Holy Grail. We get hopelessly lost and end up stuck in traffic until we're ready to give up. Piti asks a pedestrian, who confirms that there is a pharmacy near the cathedral on the main square. We are very close; it is very simple. By now, we should know what such phrases mean here: *very close, very simple*. But almost as if Haiti were out to show us that we will never guess her riddles or plumb her mysteries, a few turns, and we run into the beautiful white cathedral on a large, elegant square.

We park and set out to find a drugstore while Bill stays behind, guarding our luggage in the open flatbed. Eseline and the baby wait in the backseat. For some reason, she has not wanted to get out at any of our stops, like a caged bird that prefers the safety of its enclosure to the dangerous freedom beyond.

While Homero and Piti continue on their Dramamine mission, Eli and I peel off to peek inside the cathedral. Fifteen minutes later, when we reunite at the pickup, Homero and Eli report they could not find the pharmacy. But Bill has had better luck. A few doors down from the pickup at a small restaurant, he bought what he claims is the best cup of coffee in Haiti. (Yes, even better than in Moustique.)

But then, an unsettling incident occurs. As Bill is waiting for us, a woman comes charging across the street, berating him, an angry rant that went on and on. People stopped to watch; shopkeepers came out of their stores.

"Could you tell what was wrong?"

"She kept repeating *blan* this, *blan* that." A white man; a big, silver pickup; a young Haitian girl and a baby in the backseat — Bill could guess what she was thinking.

But he had no idea what the woman would do. Would she incite onlookers? Would she attack him? Finally, another woman with a sidewalk stand of sodas said something to the angry woman and gave her a bottle of water, which seemed to douse her anger. She went back across the street, still calling out something to Bill.

"I'm sorry," I tell him.

"It's no big deal," he says, shrugging the incident away. But from then on, whenever he regales our friends at supper parties with the story of our trip, Bill will mention this moment. It's as if he can't help mulling it over, the way the tongue keeps investigating an absent tooth. The way I keep thinking about the girl in Bassin-Bleu wanting a piece of my jewelry, and I wouldn't give it to her.

Actually, it's a surprise that this was the only racial incident, not counting the kids at the wedding who were terrified of our pale skin. Haiti's has been a race-driven history, and not just during colonial times, and not just

whites against blacks, but internally down the generations, the light-skin mulatto elite against the darker *noirs*;
the *noirs* not trusting the *griffes* or the *jaunes*.

Of course, the biggest target of hatred were the whites,
who had once been the enslavers. At the moment of Haiti's
founding as a freed nation in 1804, Boisrond-Tonnerre, one
of the signers of its declaration of independence, remarked
that the document "should have the skin of a *blan* for
parchment, his skull for inkwell, his blood for ink, and a
bayonet for pen." I'm glad that I learn about this remark
only *after* our trip to Haiti.

Before we leave Okap, we try one last time to find
a pharmacy. Several people have confirmed that a few
blocks away, up a little alleyway, we will find what we
are looking for. And sure enough, as if Haiti is determined
to surprise us once again, an eleventh-hour rescue, the dark
horse that wins the race, we find the tiny shop. It is no
larger than a hallway, a narrow slot between buildings,
easy to miss. The walls are lined with shelves to the ceiling, the shelves covered with plastic sheeting and scantily
stocked with bottles and odd items like a game of Trivial
Pursuit.

The pharmacist, a middle-aged woman wearing a top
bursting with enormous bright-pink flowers and matching

pink hoop earrings—her, you can't miss—nods. Of course, she has Dramamine pills. How many do we want? (All pills are sold piecemeal.) Three will do, Piti decides. The first one will be wasted, as Eseline swallows it right off, and ten minutes later when we're on our way, she vomits it up. But a second pill does the trick.

With our two missions accomplished, we decide to head for the border. Somehow, the incident of the angry woman seems a signal that we have overstayed our welcome. But even after we've left, we'll keep thinking about Haiti a lot, in total disproportion to the short time we spent there. Back in the States, a friend will share how she had a similar haunting reaction after visiting Brazil for the first time many years ago. "It stops you in your tracks. Mind and body. When we see a thing, what then is the obligation? That's a really big question and I worry about the answer."

Tranquila, tranquila

On the way to Ouanaminthe, I try to meditate. Instead of *Bassin-Bleu, Bassin-Bleu,* my new mantra is *tranquila, tranquila.* Stay calm. Otherwise, I'll betray our precious cargo by looking nervous. Besides, we already have proof that no matter how much head shaking goes on, little problems can be resolved at the border.

And there is a small part of me that, despite my huge doubts, wants to believe Piti. He keeps claiming that the immigration office on the Haitian side will be able to grant a temporary pass for his wife and child. "*Pero*, Piti," I keep interjecting. "You don't have any proof she is your wife. The baby has no birth certificate, proving that you are the father." Of course, all you have to do is look at that little face to see the spitting image of Piti.

We stop at the immigration building on the Haitian side. Piti gets out to inquire, while the rest of us wait in the pickup, including Eseline and Ludy. As the minutes tick by, I start wondering if Piti himself has been arrested. *Tranquila, tranquila*, I keep telling myself.

Eseline, too, is jumpy. She has been feeling fine since taking the second Dramamine. But now she is looking around, amazed by the swarming market crowd that surrounds the pickup. Everywhere you turn there are makeshift stands, wheelbarrows full of yams, plantains, oranges, big bundles of disposable diapers, cane chairs, clothing, a tangle of motorcycles, trucks, cars, carts. There are plenty of shoppers here, including many Dominicans who buy cheap merchandise on the Haitian side and then cross the bridge to sell it for double or triple the price.

Piti comes out from the small wooden building, his round, boyish face suddenly an old man's worried one. The Haitian officials have told him that there is nothing they can do. He'll have to ask their counterparts on the other side.

"Ask them for what?" I ask him pointedly.

"Can I bring in my wife and baby," he answers, as if Eseline and Ludy are pieces of luggage, not two human beings.

How could Piti think he'd get away with this? (How could *I*?) We both know Dominicans are notorious for their treatment of Haitians. In our own rural community, Haitians and Dominicans live peaceably, working side by side. But this is a rare harmony, one riddled with pointed jokes, racist comments, a blind prejudice all the more remarkable coming from those who have been victims themselves of oppression and poverty. One time a contingent of Dominican workers on the farm came to us protesting the fact that Haitian workers got the same daily wage as they. And yet, were it not for Haitian labor, Dominican agriculture, in addition to many other sectors of the economy, would come to a standstill. But no matter our interdependence, and I say this with shame, a poor Haitian can't count on having rights on Dominican soil.

But, right this moment, what I'm feeling is frustration with Piti for putting his wife and child in this predicament. It looks like we will have to turn right around and drive ten hours back to Moustique. It's either that or Piti finds a way to cross the Massacre River at night with the help of a smuggler.

"My wife, my little baby," Piti keeps pleading, as if we could work miracles.

We inch our way through the market crowd, the pickup parting the way as we go. Homero and Eli ride in the flatbed since we've been warned that anyone could grab one of our bags and run off. Not that anyone could get very far in this swarm of people, animals, and vehicles.

On the other side, the lieutenant with the gold teeth comes up to the pickup. "How was your time in Haiti?"

he asks, craning his neck to look inside the cab. I rattle on about the wedding, what a long trip it was, how we're so glad to be back. But he is not listening. His eye has been caught by the Haitian couple in the backseat. *Tranquila, tranquila,* I quiet my noisy, thumping heart, as if it were the contraband I needed to hide.

"What about them?" He nods toward Piti and Eseline.

"Oh, he's got his passport and visa." I hand over Piti's documents. "He works up on our farm," I tell the lieutenant, though technically, Piti is now the *capataz* on a neighbor's farm. But the lieutenant doesn't care about anecdotal details. He takes the passport, reviews it, then nods: everything is in order. He hands it back and looks beyond Piti to Eseline. For the first time since I embraced feminism as a young woman, I am willing invisibility on two females. May Eseline and Ludy disappear; may they be mere appendages to a husband with a passport and visa.

But the lieutenant didn't earn his gold teeth by being a blind chauvinist. "Them," he nods. "What about *their* documents?"

It is not often that I can't come up with a single word, but this is one of those times. I can't even seem to be able to tell the lieutenant the truth, which should not be that difficult, as I wouldn't have to invent it.

Once again, Homero comes to the rescue. "Lieutenant,

we have a little problem. Our worker here has his papers but his wife and baby don't. Is there a way to resolve this situation?"

Surprisingly, the lieutenant does not shake his head. This, I should realize, is a bad sign. He doesn't have to pretend to hidden cameras. There is nothing he can do to help an undocumented Haitian enter the Dominican Republic. Although he checks documents, his only authority is over vehicles—that's why he could help us with the pickup permit on our way to Haiti. We will have to inquire at Dominican immigration. But before he can let us proceed, the pickup needs to be fumigated. No telling what it picked up next door—in addition to undocumented Haitians.

A young man with a canister strapped to his back sprays each tire, then slaps the side of the pickup. We're good to go. The lieutenant is waving us through. Bill drives past the enclosed yard, under the archway that welcomes us into the Dominican Republic, and halfway down the street into Dajabón, carried along by the market crowd. No one stops us. No one comes after us. "Keep going, keep going!" I'm yelling at Bill, my one Bonnie-and-Clyde moment.

"No, no, no!" Now it's Homero shaking his head. That is a very bad idea. We might get away with not going back and paying our entry fees. But between Dajabón and

Santiago, there are at least ten military checkpoints. The minute the *guardias* spot a Haitian in the vehicle, they will ask to check passports, visas. The penalties can be dire: Eseline and the baby deported, the rest of us arrested, the pickup impounded.

"But I thought you said market day we could just whiz through the border?" I remind Homero.

"We could, you saw. But now we have to figure out what to do about the checkpoints."

What does he suggest? "*El que tiene boca llega a Roma*," he quotes a popular Dominican saying. If you have a mouth you can get to Rome. But if you are Haitian, getting into the DR is another story.

Homero, Piti, and I walk back under the arches to Immigration to get all our passports stamped, our fees paid, and—we hope—our little problem resolved. Bill and Eli stay behind with Eseline and Ludy to guard the luggage. Immigration seems to consist of two windows looking out on an inner courtyard, packed with people pressing in on all sides. I say this as a Dominican, so I don't mean to insult anyone, but we did not get the gene for waiting on line.

Homero and Piti and I join the pushing crowd, and all too soon, we're facing a middle-aged woman, who doesn't even bother to glance up. We pay our fees, get our passports stamped, and then, lightly, I broach the question.

"What can we do about a Haitian mother and her child who don't have any documents?" The woman, who has been mindlessly doing her job—collecting fees, stamping passports without bothering to corroborate faces with photos—looks up. This is one fool worth checking out. "She needs to apply for her documents in Haiti."

"But what if she's here and needs to enter now?"

The woman is shaking her head, little movements of incredulity rather than negation. She cannot believe anyone could be this ignorant. "Without documents, she cannot enter this country."

Oh yeah? Haitian mother and child are already halfway down the main street in Dajabón. But I know better than to bite the hand that might be willing to take something under the table. "What about clemency? She's a young girl; this is her first child." It's as if I'm on a talk show, trying to drum up audience support.

The woman sighs. She has to get back to work. But the fact that she doesn't bother to give me a lecture about rules being rules suggests that she knows that the rules are bendable. "Talk to one of the officials inside, maybe they can help you."

We only need to send one Daniel into the lion's den, and Homero has a good track record. In he goes to try and locate the official we dealt with two days ago. I head back to the pickup to give my fellow travelers an update, leaving Piti pacing in front of the door of the building, awaiting the fate of his wife and child.

When I return to the inner yard, Piti and Homero are sitting under an enormous shade tree whose roots probably extend into Haiti. By the looks of it, they are having a serious discussion. At first I think Homero is letting the young man down easy, delivering bad news that Eseline and Ludy will have to return home. But in fact, Homero has found out that there is a solution.

No one has stopped Eseline here at the entry, in large part because of the chaos of market day. The problem will come — as he predicted — at the checkpoints. An individual vehicle with a Haitian inside will be stopped. But there are buses that travel between Dajabón and other parts of the island, and, for a special fee, they will take a few undocumented Haitians along with other passengers. At each checkpoint, the driver then passes on part of that fee to the guards who waive checking everyone's documents.

It's actually a win-win situation because the Dominicans on the bus — whom, you'll recall, do not have the waiting gene — would not want to endure the long delays of having everyone's documents checked. As for what that certain extra fee is, Homero will have to check at the bus station down the street. First, Piti has to decide to take the risk, as in a few cases, not every crew at every checkpoint on a particular day is on board with this arrangement. But there aren't a whole lot of other options.

Piti listens carefully, and then something happens to his boyish face. A manly gravity descends on his features. It's as if he has suddenly realized what he has done. I don't mean the irresponsibility of placing his young wife and child in this predicament. I mean this is the moment when he grasps what it means to become one with his wife and child.

A friend recently told me how she asked a new colleague from Kenya if he had any family. "Yes, indeed," the man replied, "I have a large family, cousins, and aunts, and uncles, and grandparents." My friend explained that she meant family the way we use the term in this country, meaning a wife, children, the nuclear family. The man looked surprised. "But that is me."

Eseline and Ludy *are* Piti now. He nods, agreeing to take the risk for all of them. He is a boy-sized man, taking on a man-sized burden. I wish I could help him out, beam him my mantra, *Tranquilo, tranquilo,* but so far I can't say it has done much to still my own anxious heart.

Lunch with Castro at the Gran Hotel Raydan

We stop at the Gran Hotel Raydan. It's on the main drag in Dajabón, diagonally across the street from the bus station — and according to Homero, who has eaten there before, it has a decent restaurant. Out front on the patio, the few cast-iron tables and chairs are deserted. It's the hot time of day, when sensible folk are indoors in the dark, air-conditioned interior. But we're already a long ways from being a sensible bunch. We wait outside, baking in the sun, while Homero and Piti cross over to the station to make arrangements.

They come back excited, nervous, full of news. A bus is leaving in a few minutes. Initially, the dispatcher quoted twenty-five hundred pesos for taking the undocumented Eseline to Santiago. Somehow — he's getting alarmingly good at this — Homero talked the guy into accepting two thousand for Eseline. Piti, being documented, will pay the usual fare, two hundred pesos.

We hurry to get them ready. Their luggage will stay with us, but we put together a plastic bag with necessities: Ludy's bottle, a couple of Pampers from the packet we just bought, some crackers and cheese, and a bottle of water. Eseline takes the last Dramamine. Eli lends Piti his cell phone, just in case . . . We leave that sentence unfinished and skip over to a happy ending. We will meet them in Santiago. Call us the minute they get there. Eli punches my number into his cell phone and hands it to Piti.

Meanwhile, Homero, Eli, Bill and I will follow in the pickup, taking an alternate route on back roads. The fear is that if we tail the bus, the guards at the checkpoints might get nervous and decide to put on a law-abiding show for the Americanos in the pickup. Best to give the bus wide berth. Since it will be making stops along the way to load and unload passengers, we'll grab a bite at the restaurant first. We should arrive in Santiago around the same time for our rendezvous.

Homero and I accompany Piti, Eseline, and Ludy, but just as we're crossing the street, a bus is pulling out. We hurry over to the dispatcher, whose face drops the minute he sees us. Our bus just left. Furthermore, now there's an added problem. "You didn't say anything about a baby. I'd rather take ten men and as many women as take a baby."

"But why?" I'm puzzled. If the point is keeping out Haitians who will take jobs away from Dominicans, Ludy has a long ways to go before she'll be any kind of competition.

I never do get an answer as to why a baby is such a big issue. Later, Homero will surmise that the dispatcher had been willing to take twenty-two hundred because a bus was about to leave—a kind of fire-sale price. But now, with more time, the dispatcher has some elbow room to dicker. We end up paying an additional thousand pesos for the baby. The family will be on the very next bus, the dispatcher confirms, pocketing the bills.

When will that be?

"When it fills," he tells us. Meanwhile, so as not raise suspicions, Piti and Eseline should go stand out of sight at the back of the station. He gestures with his chin. He will come get them when it's time. He turns to Homero and me with a look that says, Scram.

While Homero waits, I walk back with Piti and Eseline, both big-eyed and nervous. We embrace, and something about our arms around each other, the baby in the middle, feels like a moment requiring spiritual punctuation. But what to say and to whom? It is an interesting moment when an agnostic feels compelled to lead a prayer. "Please, God, keep this family in your loving gaze. Bring us safely together in Santiago." When I open my eyes, Piti and Eseline have bowed their heads, their eyes closed, their foreheads fervently creased. Only Ludy is looking at me, a little smile playing on her lips. I suppose if there is a God, this is how he would make a visitation, on the sweet face of a child.

Back at the dark, wood-paneled restaurant in the Gran Hotel Raydan, Bill and Eli have already been seated at a table, noses buried in their menus, as if reading two engrossing novels. Our waiter, a portly, middle-aged fellow whom Homero remembers from previous visits, is named Castro. *"¿Cómo está la revolución?"* I joke with him.

Castro sighs. He must hear this a lot. He has a tired, humorless face, a man who expects the worst and is not often disappointed. He, too, has had a long day, and it's only two in the afternoon. And we are a complicated foursome: two vegetarians (Eli is a flexible vegetarian—so as not to cause a problem, he'll eat meat if that's all there is); a man who wants *chivo* as good as the one he ate in Moustique (Bill); and another who wants the delicious plate he ate the last time he was here, but he can't remember what it was (Homero). In the silence after our order is finally settled, we clink glasses.

"To Piti and Eseline and Ludy!"

A half hour later, as we ourselves are driving away from the hotel, we see another bus pulling out of the station across the street. I try to make out faces, but the windows are tinted so I can't see who's riding inside. But since this might be the bus that carries Piti and Eseline and Ludy, I give it a lucky name as it roars away, God Bless, Merci Jésus, like the tap-taps we saw earlier today.

Mèsi, Jezi, mèsi

The trip back to Santiago seems endless, and later, I figure out why: I am living two parallel lives.

In one life, I am riding in a silver four-wheel-drive 2009 Toyota pickup, stopping at some of Homero's favorite haunts, all having to do with food. In keeping with his name, Homero is the kind of companion you want to take with you on a journey. At first glance, he might not look the part — a family man with three young children, a wife, a government office job — but once he hits the road, he turns into a free spirit and bon vivant. He'll show you a hell of a good time. And when need be, he can morph into Daniel in the lion's den or undercover haggler finding you the best bargain on bribes going.

Vianela and her son, Nelson, on the road to Loma de Cabrera, sell us *dulce en yagua*, a kind of thick fudge made with milk, sugar, and any number of other ingredients (orange, cashew fruit, coconut), then wrapped in *yagua*, the husk shed by a palm tree. We buy one and a half pounds, and when she weighs the wedge on her old-fashioned hanging scale, she says, *"Le falta conciencia para ser una y media."* It lacks a conscience to be one and a half pounds. I'm taken with this roadside moralist of what amounts to ounces. And maybe because we are so close to the border,

I find myself wondering how such a fine moral sensibility would have responded to the 1937 massacre.

At Loma de Cabrera, we stop to watch *casave* being made the old-fashioned way by Luisa and her crew. It is a long, exacting, knuckle-scraping process. Now, most of the *casave* in the country is manufactured by machines in *factorías*. But here, we're back to pre-Colombian time, when the island was named Quisqueya, meaning "Mother of all the Islands." The *casave* rounds, as big as pizzas, are stacked up, appealingly irregular, which makes them look fresher, more homemade than the perfectly round packaged cakes, dry and crumbling, sold in the supermarket. Hanging from a rafter is an old leather purse, used as the cash register.

All around Luisa, boys and men are working at the different parts of the laborious process (from the peeling and washing of the yuca root, to the grinding, the first soaking, the second soaking, the forming of the cake, the patting on a *burén* — a round stone on which the *casave* is baked — the feeding of the fire, on and on). The hardest of all the jobs is the grinding, traditionally done by hand with many bleeding knuckles. (The grinding is the one part of the process that Luisa does do with a gasoline-powered grinder.) This stage is the source of the expression, *"Estoy guayando la yuca."* I am grinding the yuca, you say, when you have been working bone-achingly hard. Even with a grinder, it is a sweaty, nasty job, with the generator belching out black smoke, each yuca having to be peeled and thrust into a huge maw, the pulp collected, rinsed, the water squeezed out by hand. Again, because Haiti is on my mind, I can't help noticing how the lighter guys are up front in the retail area, doing the light work, whereas the darker boys — Haitians? — are in back, literally grinding the yuca.

This is one life I am living—stopping and chatting and learning about different artisan crafts and sampling the results. But all the while I am wondering about Piti and Eseline and Ludy. What are they going through right now? Is the Dramamine working? Has the baby fallen asleep? And more nerve-racking, have they successfully passed through the first checkpoint, the second, the third? I keep trying to call, but every time, I get the same recording: the person I am trying to reach is not available.

"He's probably got it turned off," Homero wagers. A cell phone ringing inside the bus might disturb fellow passengers. When you are breaking the law, you want to be inconspicuous.

Even on these back roads, we pass half a dozen military checkpoints. Usually it's two or three *guardias* sitting under a shade tree, shooting the breeze, a motorcycle parked nearby, just in case they have to chase down a vehicle. As we approach, one of the *guardias* stands (do they take turns?), cranes his neck, sees three white faces and one light brown man, and waves us on. But at a couple of checkpoints, as we slow down for the speed bump, the *guardias* approach and peer inside.

"*¿Cómo están?*" I ask them, friendliness being the best policy, especially with armed *guardias*.

"As you can see, we are grinding the yuca."

Sitting under a mango tree, waiting for the next bribe bus—I don't think so! But I can see, from casting a glance around them, that they haven't apprehended any Haitians. Of course, this is not the route that Piti's bus is taking, but I'm grabbing at good-luck straws wherever I can find them.

It is getting late, and a huge rainstorm is coming in. Halfway back to Santiago, the rain starts pouring down. The kind of drenching downpour where you can't make out the road ahead of you. We stop and hurriedly cover the back of the pickup with a tarp, then drive on at a creeping pace, wondering how the storm might delay the bus as well. The cell phone is getting no reception now. Luckily, I was able to get through earlier to Vicenta at my parents' house in Santiago. Please set some extra places for dinner and prepare some beds for Eli and Piti and his family. It will be too late for Eli to drive them all up to the mountain tonight, two and half hours away. They can set out fresh in the morning.

The rain stops, and as if the two things were synchronized: the cell phone rings. It's Piti! They are already in Santiago waiting at the gas station.

"Oh my god! We're at least a half hour away," I tell him. "We could hardly move in that bad rainstorm."

"What rainstorm?" Piti asks. They didn't see any rain at all on the main highway.

"You're kidding! No rain?" I ask about the checkpoints.

"No problem with the checkpoints." Furthermore, Eseline didn't get carsick. The Dramamine worked.

When we finally pull into the gas station, we spot them right away, two kids with a baby, sitting on the curb. The minute they see us, they spring to their feet, their faces radiant with relief. Even Eseline, who has been stony-faced and removed for most of the trip, comes running toward us as if we were family.

"*Mèsi, Jezi, mèsi,*" Piti keeps saying. Another weird moment for an agnostic, when a prayer she has uttered on the strength of others' faith is answered.

When we have seen a thing

W hen we have seen a thing, we have to tell the story. And yet, initially, we are dumbfounded. The return is jarring. We honk at the entrance to my parents' house. The watchman, Don Ramón, opens the tall wooden gates. He touches his Yankees baseball cap, bowing his head deferentially. It's hard to believe that this gentle, soft-spoken man, now in his sixties, used to be in the military. Did he ever accept bribes? I wonder. Or worse.

At the top of the driveway sits the big house. In the waning evening light, its shabby features aren't apparent.

The rusted ironwork at the windows, the cracked walls, the weeds coming up between the stepping stones on the way to the pool drained because of the mosquitoes — all fade into the bigger picture: this is a huge place with a large staff for just two people.

Don Ramón closes the gates and hurries up to see if we need help unloading the pickup. "And how was Haiti?" he asks politely, turning off the little radio he keeps on by his chair under the carport. The staff at my parents' house were all shocked that we would want to go to a country even poorer than ours. A rung or two below them on the ladder they are desperately climbing.

"Haiti was . . ." I look around at my fellow travelers. No one volunteers a comment. We need time to collect ourselves. In *The Odyssey*, there is a ritual way to welcome a traveler. The host settles him in his quarters, gives him time to wash up, feeds him, and only afterward comes the payback: tell me your story. For now, I settle on the generic "*Muy, muy interesante*, Don Ramón."

"*Sí, sí.*" He nods. Whatever I say, Don Ramón is usually in agreement.

Homero takes off, back to his family who await his stories. Will he tell his young sons how we resolved our little problems at the border? Or will he edit out those parts? What will the rest of us edit out? How to convey what we have seen? One thing is certain. Like the Ancient Mariner, we will feel compelled to tell the story, over and over. As a way to understand what happened to us.

But in the upstairs part of the house, in my parents' apartment, the stories are unraveling. Alzheimer's disease is breaking down their memories, undoing the narrative weave of their lives into loose, dangling threads. A stranger enters the room insisting she is our child. How can that be, when we ourselves are children? A long-dead brother returns in the eyes of a stray dog. A mirror shows a startled old woman or an old man looking back at us.

I start with the easier faces who follow me into the sitting room: my husband, Bill, whom my mother vaguely recalls; Eli, the volunteer from the United States working on our farm this year, who has been here a few times; then this young Haitian couple and their child. Piti, Eseline, and Ludy. Even to an undamaged mind, it is a complicated story to follow: borders and bribes; bad roads and great mangoes; Haitian angels and an angry woman in a town square, yelling at a white man beside a silver pickup with a black girl and her baby inside.

My father closes his eyes, exhausted with the effort of trying to understand. But my mother's good manners are still running on automatic. She smiles her company smile.

But the minute we disappear to wash up for supper, she retreats to her own bedroom. She doesn't feel well, she says, when I try to convince her to join us at the table. What she means is that she is frightened of strangers whose stories she can't comprehend even when we repeat them.

It's best not to push her. Especially at night, she can become agitated, caught in the loop of the same story: She does not want to stay in this strange house. Please, please take her home.

Piti and Eseline also don't come up for supper. Maybe they, too, are abashed, trying to make sense of this very different story: a house with enough rooms to sleep a village; a watchman guarding two elderly people who would not live to be so old had they been born in Haiti.

As I go down the stairs to fetch them, I can hear Ludy bawling away, letting it be known that she has had a hard day. That's why they haven't come upstairs, Piti explains. They do not want to disturb my parents. And after yesterday's incident at the hotel, they know better than to leave the baby by herself.

I'm grateful for their thoughtfulness. A crying baby is likely to agitate not only Mami ensconced in her bedroom but Papi sitting at the table, a vague look on his face. But he can surprise you, suddenly focusing on a detail, getting worked up, until he's in full rant. Those times, there's a little bottle in the cupboard devoted to their medications that we can give him, three drops on his tongue, if he'll let you, and if not, in a glass of water you hold up to his mouth with a straw.

On a recent visit, Eli and Bill and our son-in-law, Tom, were all having dinner at the table. My father kept eyeing them. "Where are all those men going to sleep, Pitou?" he asked my mother again and again. My older sister and I exchanged a look across the table. Our father was back in our adolescence, worried about males hitting on his daughters. Only after we made a show of parading the men out of the dining room did my father resume his meal tranquilly.

I go back upstairs and prepare a tray with two supper plates and, for dessert, two big slices of their wedding cake. A little later, I go down to collect the tray and say goodnight. By now the baby has quieted, lying on a padding of blankets on the floor.

We talk for a while, Piti explaining his plans. Tomorrow, they will head up to the mountains with Eli. At his foreman job, Piti has been promised a house for his new family by the owner he calls "*el hombre*." But so far, *el hombre* hasn't kept his promise. The problem is complicated because Piti owes *el hombre* money. I can see the worry on the young man's face. He does not want his wife and little baby living in a two-room shack with the half a dozen other Haitians who are working on the farm.

"You must take the baby in for her vaccines," I remind Piti. There is a free clinic in the nearby village. Then, since I am the godmother of their wedding, I decide to broach the topic of family planning. Unless it's too late. Maybe Eseline's nausea was actually morning sickness.

Piti looks relieved that I've brought up the topic. No, it is not possible that Eseline is pregnant. The couple have not had relations since the baby was born. In fact, he has a question for me. Can he have relations with his wife while she is nursing?

I had worried that the question would be more complicated. That I would have to plead ignorance because I've never had a child myself. But this one is easy. "Of course, you can have relations, but remember, Eseline *can* get pregnant."

"And Ludy, will she be okay?"

Now I'm the one confused. "Why shouldn't she be?"

Piti explains that he has been told that if a man has relations with his wife while she is still nursing, the baby will never learn to walk.

Later, when I tell my stepdaughter this story, she will

laugh and say, "I can bet who invented that story!" New mothers too tired and sleep-deprived to deal with horny husbands for whom a headache is no excuse. But a crippled baby might just stop them in their tracks.

"*Ay*, Piti," I say. "Somebody has been telling you stories."

But it's not Eseline he heard it from. Piti grew up mostly in the barracks, living with peers. All his education, including his sex education, came from them. I'm reminded of that boy I first saw, horsing around with other young Haitians after a day in the fields. And how far that boy has come, distinguishing himself as one of the hardest workers, promoted above Dominicans to be the foreman of *el hombre*'s farm. He has taught himself to read, write, play the guitar, compose songs. He has just married the mother of his baby girl and brought them over to live by his side. God's blessings are raining down on his life. *Mèsi, Jezi, mèsi,* all right.

Upstairs, my mother has still not come out of her bedroom. I go in to check on her. These days, whenever I enter a room and either parent gazes up, I brace myself. Will this be one of those times when they don't know who I am?

Tonight, my mother's face lights up when she sees me. "When did you get here?"

I play along — why confuse her. "Bill and I just flew in. We'll be staying with you for a week. But I hear you're not feeling well. I'm sorry."

"I'm feeling fine," she tells me, having forgotten her earlier story. "I'm so glad you found me here," she adds, patting a place beside her on the bed for me to sit down. "Tomorrow I'm going home."

"Yes, I know." I'm not humoring her. She is absolutely right: she doesn't remember this place. So how can it be her home? What's more, she will never be home again, except when — cursed, blessed disease — she forgets to remember she isn't there. "We came to help you get there."

"Thank you," she says, clearly relieved.

My father is wheeled in from the supper table, calling out, "Pitou? Pitou?" The night nurse rings the bell for Don Ramón to come help, as Papi is too heavy a weight for us to lift by ourselves. We go through the rituals of getting them ready for the night: taking out Papi's teeth, helping Mami brush hers, putting on their nightclothes, giving them their medications. For a while, we had a night nurse who insisted they pray. But mostly, it was the nurse saying the "Our Father" and "Hail Mary," my parents chiming in with the few phrases they remember, *Give us our daily bread; pray for us now and at the hour of our death; amen, amen.*

I tuck them in, join their hands together, and turn off the light. Goodnight, Pitouses, sleep tight.

Back in our room, Bill and I lie in bed talking. One of the pleasures of marriage is having someone to listen to your stories and to tell you theirs. To help you make sense of experience, weave a narrative out of the disparate threads — precisely what my parents are losing, the ability to do this for themselves and for each other.

So many things to talk about! So many details to piece together from the last three days! And more to come in the weeks ahead. Do we just keep doing this? Each day a new batch. Story as a digestive tract, a way to process what has happened and store it away in memories to recount at supper parties — nothing more? As a child, my older sister used to have a recurring nightmare: she'd be put in a room stuffed with beads she had to string together. Just when she was about to finish, the door would open, and a whole new load of beads would pour in. She'd wake up screaming and tell me the story once again. All I could think was, That's a nightmare? No monsters or murderers, no wild animals about to tear you apart? What could be so scary about endlessly stringing together beads? Now I understand.

But I'm praying to angels on high to bless us with another option: We string the beads into a ladder and climb out the window before the door opens. Story as agency, story that awakens and propels us to change our lives.

When we have seen a thing, what then is the obligation?

Bill and I talk late into the night. Finally, wearily, I ask him, "What do we do now?"

Although he often claims he is no wordsmith, Bill gives me the best answer I'm going to get. "We do what we can. We try to be generous wherever we find ourselves."

And tonight it happens — what seldom happens in a human family so scattered and stratified, so divided by opportunity that sometimes it's difficult to recognize the critter at the top as kin to the one at the bottom. Tonight, oh holy night: a disparate group has gathered like pieces of a story under one roof, all having eaten enough, all safe enough for now, all asleep or ready for sleep, except for Don Ramón downstairs with his little radio turned down low to keep him company until dawn when he, too, will get to go home.

Where Eseline's family lives

Where Charlie's family lives

PORT-DE-PAIX

Good road to Cap-Haïtien

HAUT MOUSTIQUE

BASSIN-BLEU

MOUSTIQUE

Where girl begged for medallion & rings

CAP-HAÏTIEN

Trois Rivières— without a bridge

GROS MORNE

DAJ Borde

Where Piti's mother lives

Where Eseline's godmother lives

Mango Ladies

MILOT

OUANAMINTHE

GONAÏVES

ENNERY

Our gas station, where we met up with Pablo

Little hospital with big heart

HAITI

Praying Hands

PORT-AU-PRINCE

★

PÉTIONVILLE

JIMANÍ

MALPASSE

Good road for politicos to make quick exit

Routes to Haiti & Return to Domincan Republic, 2009
Route to Dominican Republic via Port-au-Prince, 2010

ABÓN
:r crossing
town

Main Bus Route
Piti, Eseline & Ludy
took—10 checkpoints

SANTIAGO
Where Mami & Papi live

Back road where we
bought dulce en yagua
& casave

ALTA
GRACIA

JARABACOA

DOMINICAN
REPUBLIC

SANTO DOMINGO
★

BARAHONA
Our beach
hotel

——— Routes to Haiti & Return to Dominican Republic, 2009
.... Route to Dominican Republic via Port-au-Prince, 2010

TWO

Going Home with Piti after the Earthquake

January 12, 2010, the end of the world

I was talking to my sister in Santiago, the sister who has moved down there to help care for my parents, the sister of the beads nightmare, the sister who is emotive, expansive, and sometimes overreacts. It was my usual end-of-the-work-day phone call to see how the *pitouses* were doing.

"Oh my god!" my sister suddenly cried out.

"What? What?" My heart was in my throat.

In the background, my mother was crying out, a more terrified echo of my own "What? What?"

"It's nothing, Mami, just a strong wind," my sister was saying in a pretend calm voice that didn't fool me. Then, she whispered into the phone, "I think it's an earthquake.

I better go." And she was off, a click, then silence. I was left with an odd feeling. The feeling of the person who has heard the boy cry wolf before, and this time, hearing the cry, doesn't know if there is a real wolf at the door.

There was a real wolf at Haiti's door.

A 7.0 magnitude earthquake, to be exact, on the island of Hispaniola, which sits atop the boundary between two plates in the earth's crust: one of which, the North American plate, is jamming itself under the other, the Caribbean plate, which has nowhere to go. (Geology as allegory?) Felt as far away as my parents' house in Santiago, the quake's epicenter was just fifteen miles southwest of Haiti's capital, Port-au-Prince, where the clayey soil meant that the houses were like those Biblical ones built on sand. Down they came, the mansions of the rich, and the shacks of the poor, the presidential palace and many other government buildings, hospitals, schools — concrete slabs pancaking down, in a country without building codes, in a city packed with millions of people.

Months later when the final toll was taken — though *final* would be another of those wobbly words, each day or week turning up one more casualty — the Haitian government reported 316,000 dead, 300,000 injured, 1.3 million displaced, 97,300 houses destroyed. Mind-numbing figures, hard to compute unless broken down to one life at a time, one story at a time. "It's the end of the world! It's the end of the world!" one terrified young woman screamed in front of a wildly rocking camera.

Which is why, after I turned off the television with the late-breaking news, and realized that my sister had not overreacted, I called Piti. He was back to working for us. *El hombre* had not come through with the promise to build him and Eseline a little casita of their own. Instead, for months, they had been sharing a two-room hut with half a dozen Haitian workers. Piti was feeling increasingly unsettled. Eseline was distracted. Eli mentioned that every time he saw her, she was hanging out, giggling and flirting with her Haitian housemates. All those homesick young fellows, all that free-floating testosterone.

Bill and I offered Piti a job as caretaker, down the mountain, closer to town, on another piece of property Bill had bought, this time not for any humanitarian project, but for us. (Again, the marital us.) With the help of some Haitians, Bill spent ten days building a small house: four rooms, an outdoor kitchen, a back patio, a front porch. The first of January, when his term with *el hombre* was up, Piti moved into that house with Eseline and Ludy.

Piti picked up the phone after one ring. Had he heard? Yes, he had heard. They had a little radio—I could hear it in the background, sirens, a Dominican newscaster with that inflated, telenovela reporting style, which usually seems over-the-top but not tonight. The earthquake was all over the news. Horrific reports were pouring in from Haiti's capital city. Hundreds, no thousands, were believed dead — the count kept climbing.

Piti had not been able to get in touch with anybody back home: not his father in Port-de-Paix, nor his mother, nor Eseline's family in Moustique. They were very worried.

This went on for several days. I'd call and ask if he'd heard anything. Then, I'd try to reassure him with what I was hearing stateside. The earthquake had been concentrated in the Port-au-Prince area. Northwest Haiti seemed to have been spared. *"Pas de nouvelle, bonne nouvelle,"* I quoted a saying Papi had picked up during his Canada years to keep up his own spirits when there wasn't any news for weeks from home. No news, good news.

Piti did not want to contradict his *madrina*, but he was not so confident. Even if the earthquake had not been strong in Moustique, it doesn't take much to bring down a mud house with a thatch roof on an eroded hillside. No news could mean that the unspeakable had happened.

It was almost a week after the earthquake when Piti heard from a Haitian friend also working in the Dominican Republic who had gotten through to his family that everyone was fine. Piti's family. Eseline's family. Leonardo's family. Pablo's family. But since Port-au-Prince has become the only place to go in-country for jobs, each of their families had someone living in the capital — just as each family had someone working abroad — and so no one could feel completely spared.

"We are thankful and we are mourning," Piti told me. In the aftermath of the earthquake, those two feelings were so tightly woven in every Haitian heart, tears of relief could easily double as tears of grief. A sister spared but a cousin killed. A friend maimed but a brother whole. How can the heart encompass it all?

It was after the earthquake that I pulled out the journal of our journey five months earlier and read it over. I wanted to be close to Haiti in an intimate way, not the Haiti blaring all over the news, the Haiti of horrifics, the failed state, the death count rising. I wanted to hear the mango ladies laughing, and Charlie's sister sweeping the yard with a straw broom in the early morning, and the six predicators and one pastor marrying Piti and Eseline. I wanted to hold Ludy and sing her to sleep with my old Dominican lullabies. To reenter the story as a way of being with Haiti after the cameras departed and the aid folks held their conferences in First World cities, sitting at roundtables with glasses of iced water refilled by waiters from the very countries whose problems these conferences were convened to address. *The future of Haiti. The remaking of Haiti.* I didn't have any answers for Haiti or fix-it advice or even a high road to take or a moral stance for others to emulate. I just wanted to be with Haiti, and the line that kept echoing in my heart was the one from stations of the cross on Good Friday: *Walk with me as I walk with you and never leave my side.*

I didn't want to leave Haiti's side. And so I reentered the story I had written of our journey the previous summer. To borrow a metaphor from my sister's childhood nightmare, the door had reopened in the narrative I had closed, and a whole new load of beads had come tumbling in.

Wolves on both sides of the door: a very brief history of Haiti

The wolf at Haiti's door had been there long before the January earthquake.

For years we'd been hearing the sad statistics: Haiti is the poorest nation in the hemisphere, one of the poorest in the world. What happens when a natural disaster occurs in a country ill prepared to survive it? The answer was all around us in the days following the earthquake, televised scenes to break the heart and add our own emotional and moral rubble to the dust and rubble of what was left of Haiti's capital.

And the saddest part was that it was avoidable, not the earthquake itself, of course, but what had happened as a result of it. No matter how the facts were spun and the beads strung, this was not a story of a natural disaster. It was also not a story of a cursed nation whose freedom had been acquired by making a pact with the devil, as Reverend Pat Robertson unbelievably and heartlessly pronounced the day after the earthquake. It was a poverty story, a story of badly constructed buildings, poor infrastructure, and terrible public services. Just as a point of comparison: an earthquake of similar magnitude in the Bay Area in California in 1989 killed sixty-three.

How can this be? Haiti, the poorest country in the hemisphere? One of the poorest in the world? If you took a time traveler from the mid-eighteenth-century Caribbean and plopped him down in today's Haiti, he would not believe this was the same country. Saint-Domingue, as it was then known, was the world's richest colony, the Pearl of the Antilles. (Ironically, Santo Domingo next door was a destitute little colony, having been virtually abandoned by Spain for its richer, gold-laden viceroyalties in Mexico and Latin America.) In the hundred years after France acquired the western third of the island from Spain in 1697,

Saint-Domingue was producing two-thirds of the world's coffee, almost half of its sugar, large portions of its cotton, indigo, and cocoa — in short, its exports accounted for one third of France's commerce. And the fuel that powered this enormously lucrative, money-making machine was human slavery, upward of five hundred thousand enslaved West Africans, "owned" and overseen by forty thousand white Frenchmen.

Again, how can this be? How can a small fraction of a population enslave half a million people, who outnumbered them at least ten to one? In a word, terror. If we were to send a traveler from our own time back to Saint-Domingue to check out how the plantation system worked (I volunteer Pat Robertson for the mission), what a tale of horror he would tell.

Even by the standards of the day, conditions on those plantations were jaw-droppingly brutal. Field hands forced to wear masks to prevent them from eating sugar-cane; recalcitrant slaves filled with gunpowder and blown to pieces. In his book on Haiti, *The Immaculate Invasion*, Bob Shacochis quotes a journal entry by a German traveler who was horrified when the wife of his colonial host ordered her cook pitched into the oven for a mistake in the kitchen. Another entry might seem trivial in comparison, but it shows how the slavery system trickled down and deformed the human soul, from a young age on. At break-fast one morning, a colonial child announced, "I want an egg." When he was told there were none, he replied, "Then, I want two."

Finally, in 1804, after thirteen blood-soaked years of fighting, the former slaves drove out their French masters. You'd think Haiti could at last begin nation building. That the world would breathe a collective sigh of moral relief. That all those French Revolution freedom fighters, whose example had inspired the colony, would rally to her side. But as the Haitian saying goes, "Beyond the mountains, more mountains." Nation after nation shunned Haiti, re-fusing it a place in the family of nations, making it a pa-riah state. France strapped her former colony with a huge reparation payment under the threat of another invasion and reimposition of slavery. Meanwhile, the United States refused to recognize Haiti. In part, this was due to pres-sure from France, an ally, but also to fears, particularly among Southerners, that a free Black Republic right in our backyard might influence their own slaves. It wasn't until 1862, after the secession of our own slaveholding states, that Abraham Lincoln extended a hand to our neighbor to the south, and formally recognized Haiti's right to exist.

Haiti's own leaders seemed to have forgotten what they had fought for, and instead took a page from their masters, preying on their own people, declaring them-selves kings and emperors, emptying Haiti's meager coffers to fill their own pockets and fund their coronations, their castles, their revolutions, and, once in power, their mili-tary and their paramilitary militias to keep them there. Down the generations, many of Haiti's rulers grew rich but left her poor — most recently and infamously the two Duvaliers, Papa Doc and his son, Baby Doc, who plundered the terrorized country for almost three decades from 1957 to 1986. Again a small detail captures the mindless deca-dence of their regimes: Baby Doc's wife, Michele Bennett, had a refrigerated closet for storing her furs — in a tropi-cal country, no less.

Externally, rapaciousness was also the rule. Most pernicious were the loans made at such exorbitant terms that the country's financial hole just kept getting deeper and deeper. Two foreign occupations by our own United States, as well as dictatorships and military coups, often supported by the United States. Our fingerprints are all over the bruised body of Haiti.

Baby Doc was finally sent packing in 1986. From the ranks of the poor emerged a then Catholic priest, Jean-Bertrand Aristide, preaching the gospel of liberation the-ology. His wildly popular grassroots movement swept him into power in 1991, and then again in 2004. It seemed that Haiti would at last reconnect with her original revolutionary ideals and nationhood goals. But alas, both times, Aristide was ousted by coups that even by conservative analysis had the tacit approval if not outright help of the United States.

As for Aristide himself, opinions vary confusedly: from Haitians who championed him as "our modern Toussaint L'Ouverture" to Piti's negative assessment: "He did nothing for us; we only got poorer, and there was more violence because of the arming of the population." What is clear to supporters and detractors alike is that Aristide was the legitimately elected president of Haiti, and his populist agenda represented a threat to local and international beneficiaries of the old order.

It's as if Haiti's historical and political legacy were now operating on automatic, a juggernaut hurtling forward, running over the poor, the deforested countryside, the depleted economy, the disrupted nation. Add to this man-made legacy, the slings and arrows of climate and geography, including hurricanes, floods, and yes, earthquakes—though none so bad as this recent one—the wonder is that the Haitian people have survived with pride and soul intact.

That should give us pause. Notwithstanding a whole pack of wolves on both sides of her door, Haiti keeps bouncing back. After the world ends and the dust settles, heart broken, body bruised and maimed, Haiti stirs. Her spirit rallies, like that woman pulled out of the rubble after I don't know how many days, weak and lying on a stretcher, white with dust, seemingly a corpse, except that she was singing. She was singing!

It's as if Haiti *has* made a pact — with hope.

February 2010, a party and a plan

I n early February, three weeks after the earthquake, Bill and I are back in the Dominican Republic. I've stayed in regular contact with Piti by phone, and through him have kept abreast of how our Haitian friends are faring. Everyone is still reeling with shock from the disaster. Some have returned to Haiti, hoping that the reconstruction will mean jobs. But so far, no one has had any luck, since, of course, the rebuilding will not be taking place in the countryside but in the capital city, which is already packed with desperate people wanting to work.

In our own Dominican countryside, jobs are scarce. A sparse coffee harvest, a bad economy. Pablo is out of work, so we hire him for odd jobs that Piti could easily do by himself. Leonardo is off to the cane fields near La Romana, where the work is grueling. Six days cutting cane, whose sharp stalks are like knives, so that at the end of the day, his arms are full of the equivalent of little paper cuts. All this under the sweltering lowland sun. It's hard to imagine the smirking Leonardo, who didn't want to get his clothes dirty by taking his turn riding in the back of the pickup, taking on this kind of job.

"Things are very difficult," Piti admits with a sigh. It is now his habitual mode of verbal punctuation instead of the giggles of the past. The boy has become a man, a heavyhearted one.

In an attempt to raise everyone's spirits, Bill and I decide to throw a party for our Haitian friends. We'll prepare a meal, featuring a Haitian favorite, goat. Afterward, we'll have music provided by Piti and friends.

We propose the idea to Piti. What does he think?

He giggles in reply.

And so it is that a month after the earthquake, almost to the day, we are partying in the little house. It's the first time I've seen Eseline smiling since we arrived. She has been sullen, shaking her head whenever I ask what's wrong, using a few phrases I've learned in Kreyòl. But tonight, she is in her element, partying like the girl she still is. All the young Haitian men want to dance with her. I can see what Eli meant. But Piti seems unperturbed as he sings away. Thank goodness he is not a jealous man.

The party turns out to be just what everyone needs. I recall a friend guiltily confessing how after her mother's funeral, while a reception was going on downstairs, she and her boyfriend went upstairs and made love. She felt awful about it, but also strangely comforted. Death would not have the final word.

In the days after the party, Piti talks a little more about his own situation. Eseline has not been doing well. *Mal estar*, a generalized bad feeling. They did follow my advice and go to the clinic and ask for help with family planning. "So, maybe it's the birth control pills," I wager. Piti thought so, too, and he spoke to *la doctora*, who has prescribed another pill.

Over the next few months, we keep in touch with Piti by phone from Vermont. Eseline isn't getting any better. Some days she just stays in bed. But the doctors keep sending her home with a clean bill of health and another bottle of expensive vitamins. Piti doesn't know what to do except take Eseline back to Haiti. Her family has some old country cures that might work on her *mal estar.*

When I get off the phone, Bill gives me his diagnosis. Eseline is homesick. "It's been a tough few months. Lots of new things to get used to. And now the earthquake."

And so we decide to take Piti and Eseline and Ludy back to Moustique, spend a few days there, then return with Piti while Eseline stays on with the baby, recuperating.

Okay, I admit it. In this vaudeville act of who did what when and how did we get into this fix, I am the one who comes up with the idea. After last summer's arduous trip, we had both said that we were getting too old for that kind of travel adventure anymore. But these are special circumstances. Piti and Eseline are going through hard times. We are godparents of their marriage. We promised to help them out when they hit rough spots as a couple.

"You're kidding, right?" Bill exaggerates his shock. I don't know if he is more astonished by the idea of a return trip to Haiti or by his cautious wife suggesting it.

"I'm not kidding. I'm going, and you can come if you want." Fat chance I'll drive a big four-wheel-drive pickup twelve hours into the interior of Haiti on bad roads. And

I suspect that some of those cliff-hanging paths are now impassable, piled high with boulders, if not completely destroyed by the earthquake, crumbling off the mountainside and tumbling into the ravines below. Or waiting until I drive by in our pickup to do so.

"You're not going to Haiti without me!" Bill declares, just the lines I would have written for him if this *were* a vaudeville act.

But the trip will have to wait until we return in the summer, which is actually a good thing, as it'll give us the chance to plan. We want to do everything aboveboard this time, with all the right papers and supplies we need. No more trafficking with undocumented human beings and their babies. We'll stock up with supplies and also bring along gifts of food and clothes for both families.

Bill adds a side trip to our plan. If we are going to go to the trouble of driving all the way to Moustique again, then we should definitely come back via Port-au-Prince. "We should see it. Piti should see it." I should have known. Anything I come up with, Bill takes it and runs with it. It's how my writing an article about small, endangered coffee farms morphed into our owning one.

Complications

I guess it would be asking too much to have a plan go off without complication. In our intensely social, intricately interconnected, so-called Third World countries, the best-laid plans will most certainly be subject to revision, mostly the revision of addition. That is, if you plan a trip for just four of you (Bill, Piti, Eseline, me) and a baby, before you know it, there will be seven of you and a baby, and at one point during the trip, there will be eight of you, a baby, and an iron double-bed frame, which a young Haitian man had been carrying home to his new bride five kilometers away in the rain. If you have a heart and live in Haiti, or in the Dominican Republic, for that matter, your life is going to be complicated.

Actually, even if you don't have a heart, and live safely and separately and sumptuously, your life will get complicated in another direction. For example, the next time there's a revolution, your big mansion, your late-model Mercedes, and your kids with expensive First World educations will be targeted. As our yoga teacher often reminds us, when we're straining to hold our downward-dog pose, "There are two kinds of pain. The pain of doing yoga. And the pain of not doing yoga." Life is going to be complicated no matter what, so you might as well open the door and invite it into your house, or your pickup, as the case may be. Besides, someday, when you have to carry your double bed on your back, someone you once helped might give you a lift. It's the basic investment plan of the poor: save what you have by sharing it.

In addition to Bill and me, Piti, Eseline, and the baby, three more passengers join us at the last minute. The first of these is Charlie, in whose house we stayed last year in Moustique — so how can we refuse him? Charlie has been working in the Dominican Republic since last fall, but he needs to go home to attend to some business. At first he won't say what that business is, but it's a long car trip, twelve hours to his house, time to talk, and Charlie does speak a little English. We find out that he is in love. What's more, he's in love with Rozla, Eseline's sister, the very one who broke down weeping on the roadside last year when we whisked her older sister away to la République. With Piti's help, Charlie is going to make a formal declaration to her parents. This is wonderful news. Imagine! If Charlie marries Rozla and brings her to the DR, the two sisters can live close to each other. I see another wedding trip to Haiti looming in the crystal ball of the future.

Our second additional passenger is Piti's half brother, a quiet, mournful-eyed young man named Wilson (not to be confused with Willy, Piti's full brother). Wilson brings along a small bag, several sacks of staples, and a large bottle of Clorox for his mother. I'm with Leonardo on this one. A box of spaghetti makes a lot more sense.

The third last-minute passenger joins us on my invitation. Our summer volunteer, Mikaela, has just completed a month-long stay on the farm and is headed home to DC. During our farewell dinner in Santiago at my parents' house, Mikaela listens eagerly to our preparations for Haiti. I ask if she's ever been.

"It's the one thing I wish I'd gotten to do while I was here," she answers wistfully.

"So, why don't you come along?" I offer, the kind of tossed-off remark you never think someone will take you up on. Mikaela has already told us that her close-knit Italian-Irish family has missed her terribly; her two younger sisters have been counting the days until she returns; they're probably already camping out at Dulles Airport.

"Really? Can I go?" Mikaela's face is ablaze with excitement.

My heart sinks. How on earth are we going to fit all seven of us and all our stuff in the pickup? Last year we carried five passengers, six when Pablo joined us later in the trip, and the back was not piled with as many gifts and supplies. But there's no way I am going to lock the door on this lovely complication. (Sometimes it takes me a little longer to sign up for the saving-by-sharing investment plan.)

And this will turn out to be one of the best investments I could have made. Mikaela will prove to be a calm presence as problems begin to arise on this trip. (Later, we will tease Homero and Eli that they got off easy: our first trip was a piece of cake by comparison.) What's more, for five glorious days in Haiti, no one feels sorry for me and expresses their condolences that I don't have my own children. (I consider myself lucky to have two tall, blonde, beautiful stepdaughters, but I've never been able to pass them off as my own.) Everyone instantly assumes Mikaela is our daughter: Bill's blue eyes, my small size and curly hair. It's as if finally, at sixty, I've become a card-carrying member of the human-bearing race. I get totally hooked on having a daughter. Had I known it was this easy, I would have had a dozen of them.

As for our four former passengers, veterans of last year's trip: Leonardo is off working in the cane fields. Pablo is flat broke and really needing to get serious about finding work. Meanwhile, Eli is back in the States, getting ready to attend NYU law school in the fall.

Finally, there's Homero, who's still undecided whether to come along. (Where, oh where, will we put him if he says yes now?) It turns out Homero's life has gotten, well, complicated. In a word, Homero and his wife are divorcing. The wanderlusty bon vivant has won out over the family man. I worry that our trip last summer might have tipped the balance, but Homero assures me that the marriage was already in trouble.

Homero is tempted to take off for a week to return to Haiti with us. As much as I'd love to have him along — because who will get us out of any tight spots, which I imagine will be even tighter now in post-earthquake Haiti — still, I am relieved when good sense prevails, and Homero decides to stay home. He needs to spend time with his three young sons, whose fairy-tale world has come crashing down.

"He whose uncle is the mayor"

Since we're trying to do everything legally this time around, we soon encounter the maddening complications of bureaucracy. What exactly do we need to legally cross the border in our own vehicle with Haitian passengers?

I spend a day searching the Web for information, with

no luck. Finally, I turn to our problem-solver, Homero, who contacts a reliable source who maps out a process so convoluted, we would have to spend the week of our trip just getting the stamps and seals we need to take our pickup into Haiti.

Besides the bribery route, which we've vetoed taking again, and the bureaucratic route, which would gobble up all our time, there is actually a third way to get things done in our little countries: appealing to a well-placed someone you know. So common is the practice that there is a popular Dominican saying, "He whose uncle is the mayor never has to go to jail."

Bill contacts a friend in the capital who has been in the diplomatic corps. As luck would have it, this friend is good friends with the current Dominican ambassador in Haiti. Our friend cc's us on an e-mail to the ambassador asking if he'll help us out. Embajador Rubén Silié answers unbelievably promptly for a Dominican bureaucrat having to deal with communications problems in post-earthquake Port-au-Prince. He addresses me as "Esteemed Julia Alvarez," and turns me over to his assistant, the *ministro consejero*, Señor José Ortiz, who will handle everything at their end. I scan the documents Señor Ortiz requests and send them on: Bill's passport, mine, and the registration of the pickup. I wait till the fourth or fifth e-mail to ask Señor Ortiz about our Haitian friends. Can they come along? A month goes by, and it's soon mid-May, and I haven't heard back from Señor Ortiz.

I send several increasingly nudging e-mails. The subject lines speak for themselves. In late May: *Taking our pickup & friends to Haiti;* in early June: *Please let us know;* in mid June: *We'd appreciate hearing from you;* in late June: *Traveling soon — please inform us;* in early July: *Nothing from your end — do we just appear at the border?* It won't be until we are already in Santiago, the Saturday before our scheduled departure to Haiti early Monday morning, when we've already resigned ourselves to taking the under-the-table route, that I get a call from the beleaguered Señor Ortiz.

He has gotten my many e-mails, but he has been in the Dominican Republic seeing his doctors regarding high blood pressure resulting from the earthquake.

"I'm so sorry, Señor Ortiz." And I am: pestering a man who has survived the end of the world. "It's just we didn't know what to do."

"I said I would handle everything," Señor Ortiz reminds me. And he has. The consuls from both countries at the border have been notified of my coming. He will e-mail me their names. I am to ask for these dignitaries when I arrive.

"So we're all set with the pickup?"

Señor Ortiz sighs. "Our consuls at the border will take care of any paperwork."

I hesitate, wondering if I should bring up our Haitian friends again. But I can tell Señor Ortiz has had enough of me. Besides, Eseline, Charlie, and Wilson will all be staying on after we depart. Only Piti will be returning with us, and he does have his passport, though his visa has expired. But since it sounds as if I'll be traveling semi-officially, maybe my retinue will be exonerated from the usual restrictions. Here's hoping.

There is one more thing. The consuls have advised Señor Ortiz that we not travel on Monday, or for that matter on Friday. Both are market days at the border, and the crowds make the roads impassable.

No way I'm going to tell Señor Ortiz that we know all about market days, how handy they are for transporting undocumented Haitians across the border. "We don't mind at all, Señor Ortiz. It'll give us the opportunity to experience a Haitian-Dominican market day." The minute I've said it, I feel chagrined at my bold-faced lie. At our monthly *sangha* gatherings, my yoga teacher has us read the five mindfulness trainings, and the one that always trips me up is the one that goes, "I am determined to engage in right speech, to speak truthfully . . . and not to spread news that I do not know to be certain." Recently, every time I find myself inside a fib of my own making, a little spiritual red light comes on in my mind. I suppose I've made progress, as I used to lie outright and not think a thing about it.

Visiting with los pitouses

Sunday afternoon before our departure, Bill goes up the mountain with Mikaela to collect everyone: Piti and Eseline and Ludy; Wilson and Charlie. They will all sleep downstairs in the big house, so we can set off at the crack of dawn.

I stay behind to spend a little more time with my parents. What that amounts to these days is sitting around, not doing much of anything. Seldom is my father interested in a game of dominoes anymore. (Who can blame him when he always loses?) He prefers to nap, even though he has already slept until noon, when with much cursing and protesting on his part, and much cajoling and promising that he will soon be allowed to go back to sleep, we bring him to the table for lunch.

Visiting with my mother has its own challenges. Her disease has not yet reduced her to a sleeping child, but its toll on her actually frightens me more as a writer. She is losing language. Whole sheets of it have fallen away, planks of family history, elaborate stories, complex structures of syntax that she once could command in two languages. Nothing is left but a pile of pronouns, weak verbs, random words that she picks up, baffled as to what they are for. She wants to tell you . . . what was it? And if she remembers what it was, where are the words for telling it to you? I scramble to supply them, a desperate multiple choice, as she gets more and more agitated. But even when I'm sure I've nailed the one she is looking for, Mami shakes her head, no, no, no. It should come as no surprise, as even in the best of times, when her mind was sharp, my mother did not like me putting words in her mouth, especially on paper.

What she most enjoys these days is singing childhood songs and lullabies, like the ones I sang for Ludy last year on the road. She can remember bits and pieces from *"Brinca la tablita," "Arroz con leche," "Estaba la pájara pinta,"* and one of her favorites, *"Himno a las madres,"* a sappy hymn to mothers, impossible to sing dry-eyed. Old roles die hard.

Today, she and I sing along with a CD I found of Dominican childhood songs. Finally, needing a rest, I bring up that Bill and I are going on a short trip tomorrow. "We'll be back next Saturday. Just so you know."

"A trip?" she asks. "Where?"

"Actually, right next door." Do I tell her? Why is it even at this late age, I continue to be a child, wanting my mother to know what I'm up to? "We're visiting Haiti."

"Haiti?" She shakes her head vehemently. "You don't . . . you can't . . . I mean . . ." Her hands fly up, gesturing manically, as if she could grab the words she wants out of thin air.

I can tell what has happened. She has seen the footage on television: the earthquake and all the subsequent updates.

"Oh, Mami, don't worry. Where we're going is a part of Haiti where there wasn't an earthquake." It's a half-truth, since we will be visiting Port-au-Prince on our way back from Moustique. But I've already upset her enough.

"Where . . . how will you . . . you know . . ."

Most times I know what she means, but this time I'm stumped. The best thing to do when this happens is change the subject, so as not to frustrate her further. I ask her if she remembers the lullaby about the baby who grew wings and flew away. I start singing it, and she joins in.

That night, after dinner with our fellow travelers and my sister, Bill and I say our goodnight to the *pitouses*. We won't wake them tomorrow, as we're leaving so early.

As we enter the room, Mami's face lights up. She points an index finger at Bill and bursts out laughing. "You . . . you . . . I know you . . ." She has recognized him. It makes Bill's day.

"And I know *you*, Mami," Bill laughs back. "And I know Papi, too," Bill adds, as my father has opened his eyes from his side of the bed, wondering, no doubt, about this male intruder in his all-female family. "We're a family," Bill adds. "Thank you, Mami and Papi, for letting me join your family."

"Oh, you're very welcome." My mother giggles flirtatiously, still vulnerable to male praise. How is it my spouse, who hasn't lived with this old woman and man half as long as I have, always knows the right things to say to them?

Later, when I tell Bill that I messed up and told Mami that we were going to Haiti, and that she got all agitated, he reassures me. "She's already forgotten about it. I wouldn't worry about it."

But I do worry. Perhaps it's why that night I dream I am on a trip with Mami, just her and me, in the silver pickup. Our destination is a house that looks like the houses in Moustique, where a party has assembled, friends, family, even her daughters who can't have been born yet, because when I turn to tell her we've arrived, my mother is the young woman I know only from her wedding photographs.

July 5, on the road to Moustique again

Packing up the pickup

Very early Monday morning, we wake up our fellow travelers, sleeping in scattered bedrooms in the downstairs part of my parents' house: Piti and Eseline and the baby; Wilson and Charlie; Mikaela.

An hour and a half later, we still haven't left. With the help of Piti, Charlie, and Wilson (I have enough sense to steer clear), a frustrated Bill is still trying to figure out how to fit all the supplies, gifts, and luggage into the pickup, and leave enough room for five of us to ride inside with the baby, and Charlie and Wilson in back. Each time Bill successfully jigsaws the sacks of rice and ground corn and oatmeal and beans, the large canisters of oil and vinegar, the dozens of cans of tomato paste, bags of coffee, bars of chocolate, boxes of spaghetti and macaroni, and two duffel bags stuffed with clothes, it turns out he has forgotten a suitcase or the bags of brown sugar or the six *racimos* of plantains or the damn bottle of Clorox. The sun rises. My beloved is sweating.

At one point, my sister comes down the front steps in her nightgown, wondering why we haven't left at the crack of dawn. She hangs out with us, playing with Ludy, and serving up bowls of oatmeal to whoever is taking a break from helping Bill solve the luggage jigsaw puzzle. We advise Eseline not to eat and to take the Dramamine I remembered to bring with me. In an inspired moment, which we will later recall with gratitude, my sister goes up to the kitchen and brings down a bunch of plastic shopping bags, "in case the Dramamine doesn't work."

Finally, the gifts and supplies and luggage are piled high in the back. Wilson and Charlie climb on top. The rest of us pose in front of the laden pickup, and my sister snaps a picture. At the bottom of the driveway, Charlie climbs down to open and close the gate behind us, as Don Ramón already left for home hours ago at the crack of dawn.

At the border

We arrive at Dajabón, and the consuls were right. Neither Bill nor I recall the market being this busy the last time around — maybe because it was Friday, midafternoon, and business was winding down.

Soon we find ourselves trapped in a river of traffic; the one road to the bridge-crossing is jammed with trucks, handcarts, mule carts, *motores*, people. No way we can move forward, or backward, as the crowd has closed behind us.

Our cell phone rings. It's one of the consuls, who got the number from Señor Ortiz. There's a welcome committee at the border that's been waiting for over an hour for our arrival. Where are we?

I explain that we are a couple of blocks away. But we're not moving.

Where is your escort?

What escort?

The military escort that was supposed to meet us at the edge of town and open up the way for us. What kind of a car are we driving?

Car? "We're in a pickup." I hear a pause at the other end before the information is repeated, "They're in a pickup, silver, the husband is driving." He must be talking to the soldiers on a walkie-talkie or another cell phone. Something in his tone tells me that he now understands why the military escort missed us. They were probably expecting a Mercedes driven by a chauffeur.

Since we can't turn around and drive back to connect with our escorts, I climb out to look for them. The traffic is two-way on this packed thoroughfare, but I seem to be walking in the wrong lane. Waves of people keep carrying me backward. Carts threaten to overrun me. Finally, I spot four boys — really, they don't look more than sixteen — dressed in camouflage with rifles and helmets. It's as if we're to be escorted into a war zone, not just into Haiti.

"Hi," I call to them. "Are you our escorts?"

They look me over. I can see they don't believe I'm the important person they are supposed to escort to the border: black jeans with the bottoms already muddy, clunky Birkenstock-type sandals, a blouse missing a button, hair needing a comb.

What finally convinces the soldiers is when I dial the consul on the cell phone I thought to bring along. "I've found them," I report. "We're on our way."

It takes us over forty minutes to travel the two blocks. The soldiers push ahead, on foot, two on each side of the pickup, moving people to the edges, clearing the way.

Every few feet we have to stop where two or three trucks, parked across the road, are blocking any passage. The soldiers grow weary and mean. One of them gets rough with a young Haitian boy, shoving him out of the way, sending him flying. I roll down my window and shout for him to stop. He can't hear me. I call to his buddy, who is closer by, but he has whipped out his cell phone and is reading his text messages.

"Roll up your window!" Bill shouts at me, as yet another basket of fly-laden fruit is thrust in at us.

The river of people is curious about this big silver fish getting through. They press their faces on the closed windows, motion to the wares they are carrying. Mikaela giggles nervously and waves. Soon we're all waving, Piti wagging Ludy's little hand. Only Eseline looks blank-eyed, dizzy. The Dramamine is not working.

But we can't open the windows for her to throw up, not in this crowd. Thank goodness the plastic bags are handy.

Finally, we're driving under the archway and into the inner yard where the welcoming committee is waiting in the hot sun. There are a couple of military men in uniform, the Haitian consul incredibly dressed in a full suit, and two Dominican consuls, one in a jacket, the other in a more reasonable guayabera, which probably looked fresh two hours ago. I introduce myself, Bill, Mikaela, our Haitian friends. A reporter from a paper in the capital steps forward, wielding a microphone. His photographer gestures for us to stand snugly together so we can all fit in the picture.

"What do you have to say to us, Julia Alvarez, about Haiti?" the reporter asks.

Out of the depths of some college survey course, or maybe the research reading I've been doing, arises a remark made by José Martí. "Haiti and the Dominican Republic are the two wings of a bird that can't fly unless they work together." Later, I will discover that my memory only half-served me: José Martí did indeed make the remark, but he was speaking of Cuba and Puerto Rico, not Haiti and the Dominican Republic.

The members of the welcoming committee are each asked, in turn, what they think. They all elaborate the same sentiments. Haiti and the Dominican Republic, two wings, two brothers, two nations on one island. The rhetoric has never been the problem.

The sun is bearing down on us. The Haitian consul, who is carrying a cell phone in each hand, periodically brings one up to his ear and starts talking. Everyone has other appointments to get to, much more important fish to fry than this ragtag group of travelers. But the reporter needs something juicier. Something that will make the people back at the home office in the capital think it was worth sending him and a photographer five hours north to interview a writer who doesn't look very important.

"So what will you be doing in Haiti?" the reporter asks.

I explain I'm just visiting the families of some Haitian friends whose wedding I attended last year.

Later, a friend will send me a link to the article that appeared in *Hoy*. How I came to the border to collect facts for a history book I am writing on Haiti and the Dominican Republic. It seems I'm not the only one spreading news that I do not know to be certain.

The speaking landscape

It's well past noon before we finish with the farewells at the border. But before we can proceed on our trip, Piti has several errands to run in Ouanaminthe.

I'm feeling impatient, as I know all about errands in our part of the world — they can take all day. With four months of planning, Piti was supposed to have everything ready at his end. "Kids are like that," Bill reminds me. They wait till the last minute; they figure you'll take care of stuff for them; they read their text messages in-stead of doing their crowd control. Bill doesn't have to add what we've both realized over the course of the last year. Piti — and by extension, Eseline, and Ludy — are now our kids. Maybe it's not as easy to have them as I thought.

Piti directs Bill to a side street where we park in front of a compound of small concrete houses surrounded by a stone wall. This is where the moneychanger/visa procurer/border smuggler has his operation. Piti needs to exchange some pesos for gourdes to leave with Eseline. He and Bill disappear inside, and after about ten minutes, I wonder if they've been kidnapped or what.

I climb out of the pickup, ready to go in search of them, when I happen to gaze across the street. BANQUE PATIENCE, the sign on a shop reads. These *banques* — which are not banks, as I first assumed, but places where you can buy lottery tickets — will turn up everywhere, Patience being a popular name for them. Patience! Okay, I tell myself, climbing back into the pickup. Minutes later, Bill and Piti emerge from the gated compound.

Throughout this trip, this will keep happening. A sign on a store front, the logo on a T-shirt, graffiti on a wall will catch my eye with a pointed message. After sev-eral occurrences, I'm convinced that Haiti is speaking to me. Most often it's the tap-taps with their prominently displayed names. Just when I need a reminder, a tap-tap named CONSCIENCE will go by, or L'AMOUR DU PROCHAIN (Love Your Neighbor), or HUMILIACION, or, at the nadir of the trip, when Bill and I are bickering, a tap-tap pulls up alongside us with the name in English — I kid you not — MY LOVE ON THE LINE.

Next stop is a cell-phone store to buy a chip so that Piti's phone can work in Haiti. The problem we soon encounter is that the stores don't really have inventory, just odds and ends that fit one brand and not another. When we finally find a chip that we're told will work, we decide to try it out before we leave the shop. I dial Señor Ortiz, who has returned to Port-au-Prince, to tell him we are now in Haiti.

He answers with caution in his voice. Since I heard his title, I've been wondering what exactly a *ministro consejero* does. Now I know. A *ministro consejero* deals with people like me. Pesky faux-nieces and -nephews, who are not even related to the mayor, asking for favors.

I thank him for our nice welcome at the border. How right he was about market day. And because this is my last chance to ask, I mention that we have a Haitian traveler whose visa has expired. I don't know if the silence at the other end means Señor Ortiz's blood pressure has again shot up or that the chip has stopped working. But finally, I hear his long sigh. "What is his status?"

Status? I have no idea. I ask Piti. He has no idea. "We have no idea," I tell Señor Ortiz, though I suspect the answer is "illegal." Then mercifully for both of us, the phone signal drops. About ten minutes later, as we're driving out of Ouanaminthe, the phone rings. It's Señor Ortiz. There is a person at the consulate in Port-au-Prince who will try to help us acquire whatever visa it is that Piti will need to reenter the Dominican Republic. He gives me her name. But we must be there first thing on Friday morning, as the office closes midday and will not reopen till Monday.

"Poor guy," I say, handing the phone back to Piti. I swear I'll never do this again. It's no fun being the cause of somebody's high blood pressure. Part of the reason I haven't enjoyed our farm project half as much as Bill is that since I have the language, I'm usually the one delivering the bad news, firing the drunk manager, pestering the *ministro consejero*.

The little hospital with a big heart

Our first stop is Milot, twelve miles southwest of Cap-Haïtien. We're scheduled to visit Hôpital Sacré Coeur, a small Catholic hospital where several friends who are physicians have been on mission trips. Bill was planning to volunteer even before the earthquake, now with more reason. We had told our contact that we would arrive by ten, so Bill can check out the facilities for a future trip. But by the time we pull up in front of the hospital, it's close to midafternoon.

The hospital used to be a small sixty-eight bed facility. But in the days after the earthquake, it was turned into a triage center for the trauma victims pouring in from the capital six hours south. Both the hospital and the town vowed not to turn anyone away. As a result, the hospital now has over four hundred beds, the excess housed in tents across the street, and the town is packed with refugees and the families of the victims.

This far out—almost six months since the earthquake—many of the patients are in rehabilitation, learning to use their artificial limbs. One boy is doing his physical training exercises with the help of a perky, blond physical therapist from California. My eyes are drawn to his artificial limbs, so it isn't until I look up that I notice the T-shirt he's wearing: FLY, it reads, then an acronym, no doubt some travel company. T-shirts, too, begin to join the landscape conversation. On our fourth day in Haiti, en route to Port-au-Prince, when our spirits are flagging, and Bill and I are at it again, we will pass a woman wearing a T-shirt that reads: STOP BITCHING: START A REVOLUTION.

Everywhere, we spot volunteers in blue and green scrubs, nurses and doctors and occupational therapists, from the States, from Europe, from Russia, Australia. A middle-aged nurse from Ireland greets us, her hazel eyes sparkling with energy. She has been here for three months, and no, she is not going native, she jokes when she sees me eyeing her graying cornrows. "But let me tell you one of my little charges got a treat, playing with what she calls 'doll's hair.' "

Outside the children's wing, we find three elementary schoolteachers from California, painting murals of trees and flowers and butterflies. They usher us inside to show off the cheerful murals in the ward. I come upon a skinny toddler, who doesn't seem to have anything wrong with him — no missing limbs, no bandaged wounds. But unlike the children in the other cribs, he has no mother or other family member attending to him. I linger at his side, looking into his eyes, making a connection. When it's time for us to go, he wails for me to stay. How on earth do people do this?

Piti joins us for part of the tour, Wilson spelling him with Eseline at the pickup. We've all grown quiet with a kind of reverence, and not only because we're in the presence of suffering, but also of goodness. People have flocked here for the last six months to help. A town with very little has opened its doors to share with those who have nothing. People can be amazingly kind. Why are we so surprised? That is a victory for the cynics we also carry inside us: how we often expect people to be otherwise.

Blowout in the Gardens of the Sea

We must have some kind of bad karma with Madame Myrième that consigns us to making bad entrances at Les Jardins de l'Océan. Again, we roll into Cap-Haïtien at the end of a long day, when we're scruffy, dirty, and out of sorts.

"Bonsoir, Madame, *comment t'allez vous?"* I dust off my high school French. Homero is not here to translate, and I know Madame does not speak *anglais.*

Madame rattles off a greeting.

"Nous avons retournés avec nos amis," I say, mangling the accent.

Madame nods. She can see that we have returned, me, Bill, the young couple and the baby.

"Tell her we need four rooms," Bill instructs me. "Ask her if she can give us a special rate."

Is he kidding?! I've about used up all my French. *"Quatre chambres"* is as far as I can take us.

All rooms are eighty-five dollars a night, Madame announces. She must've understood Bill's English. With an added surcharge if more than two stay in a room, she adds, eying Wilson and Charlie and Mikaela.

Bill shakes his head. Like we're really going to get

back in the pickup and go hotel bargain hunting at this hour.

Madame closes her account book, as if she's done for the day. Two strong wills face each other off. But it's no contest. The lady with the hotel and a French restaurant in the lobby is the winner. Give it up, Bill.

We take the rooms at Madame's regular price, but the contest is not over. At supper, Bill ends up sitting at the head of the table, where he faces Madame at her post across the room in the lobby. The waiter did not take the feng shui course on where to seat dinner guests to mini- mize negativity.

It's actually because of the waiter that the blowout happens. A thin, bespectacled young man, who is eager to please, he deserves a nice tip. But when the credit card slip comes, Bill is miffed that the total has already been filled in with no space left to include a tip. He sends the slip back. He wants a new one written up.

The waiter returns, old slip in hand. Madame cannot write another bill because the credit card slips are num- bered, and she must account for each one.

Bill pushes back his chair and marches over to Ma- dame's post to give her a piece of his mind. Next thing I know Bill is tearing up the credit card slip, and Madame is calling him something that was never on any vocabulary list back in high school French class. Meanwhile, Mikaela and I are looking at each other with raised eyebrows, probably thinking the same thing: Unless Bill calms down, we're going to find ourselves sleeping on the street tonight.

Bill does calm down, later in our room, after he has had a chance to fume, after I agree with him that patrons should be able to write in tips on their credit card bills. But letting his anger have its day, well, it's just giving in to the worst side of his nature.

"I do it all the time," I'm quick to assure him, just so he doesn't have to remind me that I do it all the time. Why just this morning if it hadn't been for a sign across the street from where we were parked, I would have stormed the smuggler's compound in search of him and Piti.

Bill doesn't get what I'm saying. "What sign?" So I tell him about the landscape speaking to me, the PATIENCE BANQUE, the FLY T-shirt, the PEACE AND LOVE HOTEL. Even the GIV beauty soap I just saw in the bathroom should remind us both of how to behave toward each other.

My beloved is now quietly watching me, as if he's wondering if he doesn't have bigger problems on his hands than Madame Myrième. A wife going off the deep end in Haiti.

I know there's probably a pathology out there for people who seriously believe the world is winking at them, sending them secret messages. That's not what I mean. I explain about details in the landscape serving as reminders. Nothing more weird than that.

When we return to the subject of Madame, it's now a different Bill, pissed off at himself for giving in to his anger and frustration.

"So, what should I do?" It's so seldom Bill asks me what he should do, I savor the moment a moment. I'm reminded right then and there why I love him. He's never a done deal. He has agreed to live with me, both of us works in progress, as individuals and as a couple.

"Just apologize," I tell him. "It won't take anything away from you, really," I add, because I see the annoyance returning on his furrowed brow.

Next morning we're downstairs, surprisingly, before Madame. Maybe she had a bad night fuming about her boorish guest. When she does appear, Bill ducks his head and glumly finishes his breakfast. He's not going to do it, I'm thinking. But as we head out of the dining area and upstairs to pack, Bill peels off to the kitchen doorway where Madame is giving orders. I see her scowl as he approaches. I hear him say, "I'm sorry." And then—why he asked me last night how to say it in French, he adds, *"Pardonnez-moi."*

Madame smiles gruffly in reply.

July 6, on the road

Maybe a little, yes

The road to Ennery is as long as I remember it. But the good news is that it's only as bad as it was last year. No avalanches of rocks caused by soft tremors felt inland during the earthquake. No further horrible disrepair, because the transportation department can't function since the government building in which it was housed collapsed. When I remark on this to Piti, he laughs. Even before the earthquake, the roads were very bad.

I've been on the lookout for the mango ladies, and not just because we're all ready for a snack. Bill has been swearing up and down—with an adamancy that makes me want to prove him wrong—that the mango ladies' stand is after Ennery. I say it's before. As the kilometers roll on, and still no mango ladies, I know I should probably concede. But since we set out this morning, every time I've mentioned an upcoming landmark to Mikaela, Bill has corrected me. It is beginning to annoy me.

We spot an old, toothless woman with a basket on her head. When we pull over, the woman's face lights up with such joy. She has already made a sale as far as I'm concerned. But the fruits she shows us turn out to be the scrawniest specimens we've ever seen. They actually look unhealthy. "They are very good, very sweet," the old woman assures us. We end up buying two anorexic pineapples and a bunch of finger-sized bananas to snack on until we can get our hands on some mangoes. "After Ennery," Bill quips. If the backseat travelers weren't there, I'd take one of those skinny pineapples and whack him over the head with it.

Poor Eseline is sick all the time now. I dread to think of her trip back on public transport when she returns to the Dominican Republic after her cure. As to when that will be—there seems to be a difference of opinion. Piti wants Eseline to stay until he can come get her himself. But the soonest he can be back is Christmas, six months way.

Sick as she is, Eseline won't hear of it. A good sign, I'm pleased to see. Bill might be right in his diagnosis that the marriage is not in trouble. Eseline is just homesick. But she also doesn't want to be parted from her husband. She is beginning to like the "good life" in Jarabacoa. Since our February trip, Eseline has been riding into town with the baby on back of the motorcycle we helped Piti buy. Jarabacoa has got to be more stimulating for a young person than the remote countryside of Haiti.

Eseline actually looks different, more stylish in her store-bought clothes with a snazzy handbag and a little faux-leather cap. Some of this is may be my doing, picking out items for her in the sales racks of our local T.J. Maxx. But it isn't until her godmother in Gros Morne runs her hand through it that I realize Eseline has straightened her hair. In one photo with her braided little cousins, I catch an increasingly familiar gesture: Eseline swinging her doll hair.

Eseline wants to come back with Charlie or Wilson when they return to the Dominican Republic in a few weeks. But Piti is noncommittal. Eseline scowls at him, eyes narrowed. Given my growing frustration with Bill, it's helpful to be reminded that all couples have their rough patches. "I cannot say / that I have gone to hell / for your love," William Carlos Williams writes to his wife in "Asphodel, That Greeny Flower," "but often / found myself there / in your pursuit."

We stop at Ennery, at "our gas station." We've made good time, so we're feeling expansive, able to take the time to sit down and eat some of the snacks we brought along. The old restaurant has been boarded up, and a new one is under construction. The wrought-iron chairs and tables have been brought down to one side of the pumps. Most of them are occupied, including one table full of young people, all of them watching us.

Bill and Piti go up to a makeshift shack where refreshments are being sold. The rest of us take what chairs we can find around the only unoccupied table.

Piti returns with refreshments, sodas, and curious little plastic sacks you suck on full of cold water. When Bill joins us with his Prestige, he's disgruntled again. It turns out that the woman in the shack wouldn't give him back his change. He waited as she took other orders and just ignored him. Finally, Bill held out his hand, and the woman reluctantly slapped down his change.

"What's with her?" Bill asks me, as if I should know.

Piti shrugs. "Some people, they are like that."

Charlie is Mister Cool behind his reflector glasses. He says nothing. But he looks like he is thinking about it.

So, I put the question directly to him. "You think it's because we are white?" Behind the glasses, who knows what Charlie's eyes are doing. But in a calm voice, like a sibyl pronouncing, he says, "Maybe a little, yes."

Maybe a little is a lot of progress as far as I'm concerned, given our two countries' divisive racial history.

Piti cuts the two pineapples with a blunt machete, dicing them deftly into cubes.

The old merchant lady was right. This is the sweetest pineapple we have ever eaten! We each take a few chunks, then pass the paper plate around to our fellow diners at the other wrought-iron tables.

The woman at the window has been watching the plate making the rounds. When it comes back to our table, she gestures for me to bring her up a piece. "You're going to give her some of our pineapple?" Bill can't believe it.

"You bet." I go up to the window and hold out the plate. She scouts out the remaining pieces and takes the biggest chunk. Smart cookie. I laugh, she laughs. A little while later, I'm back at our table, and I glance her way. The woman nods at the one chunk remaining on the plate.

I get up again, Bill meanwhile shaking his head in mock disapproval. By now, he's enjoying how things have turned around. At the counter I hand her the paper plate. Then I stretch out my hand, palm up. She knows what I want and gives me a high five before popping the last piece of pineapple into her mouth.

Two Mountains never meet, but two people can meet again

After Ennery is where the road turns dusty, the tires of the pickup kicking up clouds of white powder. This time around, we don't have the option of taking everyone inside the cab with us. Charlie and Wilson cover their noses and mouths with kerchiefs like guerrilla rebels trying to safeguard their anonymity.

What is keeping us all going is the gratifying thought of the reunions that lie ahead: Piti with his mother, Charlie with Rozla and his daddy, Eseline with her family, and Ludy with everybody. *"Dos montañas no se juntan pero dos personas sí,"* the Dominicans like to say, a saying that also exists in Kreyòl: *"Dé mònpa janm kontré, min dè moun vivan kontré."* Two mountains never meet, but two people can meet again.

The reunion with the mango ladies is a sweet foretaste of what awaits us in Moustique. As we pull over and dismount, I with Ludy in my arms because Eseline has been too sick to hold her, the faces of the mango ladies light up. They laugh, nodding. We meet again. Two mountains can never do this, but two or more people can.

Forgotten is my annoyance with Bill, which momentarily flared up when he pointed out that the mango ladies were just ahead, like he'd said. This moment's delight casts its wide net over whatever marital rough patch we've hit on this road trip. The hours and days of our lives tick on relentlessly, and death will sunder us all, even me and my annoying beloved. I do not need to kill him. Time, alas, will do it for me.

We make our purchases, Ludy greedily reaching for one of the mangos to gnaw on. This, too, delights the ladies. A hungry baby satisfied. Not something that can be taken for granted in this area of rural Haiti.

We pile back in the pickup, honking and waving goodbye. The stop has raised all our spirits. Even Eseline has come out from under the pall of her car sickness. The Dramamine she took at lunch is taking effect. That and the imminent homecoming. The closer we get to Moustique, the happier she becomes. *"Chichí, chichí,"* she points out the window to the baby, giggling. *Chichí* is the Dominican word for baby, an interesting choice, given that Eseline has refused to speak a word of Spanish during her months in the Dominican Republic. But now, she is the returning daughter, showing off what she has learned on her travels.

As we approach Gros Morne, Piti asks if we can make a quick stop. Eseline wants to say hello to her godmother. We detour off the main road, twisting here and there, into little alleyways that don't seem wide enough for a car. Finally, Eseline motions for us to pull over under a scrawny tree. We'll have to walk the rest of the way to her god-mother's house.

As we are disembarking, two little girls come racing around the corner and hurl themselves at her. Their mother trots behind them, her arms spread. She rocks Eseline in an embrace so violent, it's a wonder *chichí* isn't knocked off her mama's arms. The godmother pulls back to take in her goddaughter's full measure, shaking her head, pleased with what she sees. Eseline has put on weight. She's look-ing so stylish in a bright red top with a "diamond" clasp, a glossy tan skirt, and a mustard-colored handbag. But what draws the loudest exclamations: her hair!

I remember the godmother from the wedding. She had been ready to step in had Madrina reneged on her promise and gone off to the gathering of the Thirteen Indigenous Grandmothers instead. Back then, the godmother seemed serious to the point of unfriendliness, perhaps upset with these strangers who would be taking away her goddaughter after the ceremony. Now, she is all smiles, the space between her two upper front teeth making her look even jollier.

The godmother remembers me, Bill. She looks Mikaela over. Then points to me, to Bill. I nod. The woman laughs. She can tell: Mikaela is our daughter.

The two little girls, joined by a third, spirit Ludy away, like a new toy. We follow them down a narrow passageway into a tiny house. The first room we enter is occupied by a large bed, where the girls have set Ludy down and given her a bald, legless, white-skinned doll to play with. Their new, live doll playing with their old, worn-out one.

We are taken through a second middle room to a third room — and that's the whole of the house. Some discussion ensues; I think about whether we are going to stay and eat. We seem to have lost our translators; Charlie and Piti have lagged behind our excited little clutch of women. The godmother uncovers a pot of plain white rice, perhaps just so Eseline can look it over, then wraps it up in a cloth for her to carry.

Piti and Charlie join us, beaming, obviously happy to be among their own. Charlie especially, for good reason. It turns out that Rozla has moved to Gros Morne to study, and this is the very house where she is living!

Unfortunately, Rozla won't be back from her classes until late afternoon, after we're gone. But no matter, Charlie will be seeing her next week, hopefully with permission from her parents to propose to her.

We hate to cut short the reunion, sweet as it is, but it is past three, and several hours of travel await us. Reluctantly, the little girls release Ludy, and we head back to the truck. I put my arm around Eseline, a not infrequent gesture of affection on my part. For the first time, Eseline reciprocates and throws her arm around me. I claimed her a year ago when she married Piti. But it's not until this moment that she has claimed me.

Connecting to a Higher Power

W e're back on the main road, nervously watching the waning light in the late-afternoon sky. And it's not just the sun setting; thunderclouds are massing in the distance. It seems the height of selfishness to wish for no rain in parched, drought-ridden Haiti. But not only will our luggage get soaked and some supplies damaged, but in the eroded landscape of Haiti, downpours often result in flash floods.

"What'll we do?" I ask Bill quietly, so as not to alarm anyone.

"Nothing at all we can do," Bill responds. So much for not alarming your wife.

I scour the desolate landscape for some comforting T-shirt message or store sign. But Haiti has stopped speaking to me. Unless you count what happens next as another sign that this trip is going to require more from me than I want to give it. Up ahead, a crowd is milling around two trucks, each one facing in the opposite direction. Somehow, in passing, their rear sides rammed into each other, and got stuck together. Since the two trucks take up the entire width of the road, no one can get past this roadblock.

The crowd, mostly men, shout advice or look on, shaking their heads. Behind us, cars and motorcycles pile up, and we can see the same stopped traffic on the other side. How will any of us get to where we are going tonight?

Piti, our diligent problem-solver, starts asking around,

but there seems to be no other road to Bassin-Bleu. A half hour goes by, an hour. Evening is coming on. The only solution I can see is to head back to Gros Morne and ask Eseline's godmother if we can crash at her house. Not a great solution once I do the math: one bed divided by too many of us.

A heavyset guy with a big voice has taken charge. He issues instructions to rock the two trucks in order to disengage them. To no avail.

I decide to ask him if there isn't some local authority we can call on. "Police?" I ask. A stupid question.

The man looks at me for a long moment. *"Polis?"* he finally snorts, rubbing his fingers together. Money is the only thing that will draw the police anywhere. *"Polis,"* he keeps repeating, more angrily each time. Then he points upward and pronounces, *"Bondye."* God is the only one who can help us.

So maybe this is the message? Connect to a higher power. I head back to the pickup, whose four doors have been thrown open to air out the inside. In the backseat, Eseline couldn't wait for her first taste of home cooking. She has raided the pot her godmother gave her. I'm about to remind her that she shouldn't eat or she'll get carsick. But that's right, we're not going anywhere.

Mikaela has followed me back to the pickup. On the

road for hours, we've talked about any number of things, including yoga and meditation. Mikaela has expressed an interest in learning how to meditate. "We could try now," I suggest. Never mind that this is the worst of circumstances: surrounded by a noisy, frustrated crowd, with thunder rumbling in the distance, fears of flash floods in at least one of our heads. I walk Mikaela through the basics: close your eyes, follow your breath, as thoughts enter your mind, observe them, let them go.

We do maybe ten minutes of this before we're interrupted by the men coming back to the truck. Piti has found a guide who says he can show us a detour to the other side of the road. But I thought there were no other roads? This young man says there is a way to get there from here. The caveat is that Piti does not know him, and so we might possibly end up stuck somewhere else, or, worst-case scenario — courtesy of my own runaway thoughts — we might be led into an ambush. I look Piti in the eye. It's that moment when you let a grown child know that the roles have reversed. He will now take care of you. "Piti, whatever you think. I trust your judgment."

"I checked his identification. He used to be a chauffeur. I think he can help us."

And so it is that after an hour of waiting, we climb

into the pickup, the young sweet-faced guy coming inside with us, Piti translating. We make a U-turn and head back toward Gros Morne, until we come to an almost dry riverbed we crossed earlier. There, we veer off the road, down the side of a bank, and into the riverbed. We drive on it, twisting where it twists, for about three kilometers. If those thunderclouds let loose, we are in big trouble. In fact, it's how flash floods happen: dried-up riverbeds suddenly flooding with waves of churning, muddy water, carrying everything in their path. (I've seen them on the Weather Channel.) I remind myself to breathe.

Only when we see a truck coming toward us in the opposite direction, a truck Mikaela recognizes as having been on the other side of the two-truck roadblock, do we let out a sigh of relief. If that vehicle has made it here, then we can get there, and vice versa. We blink lights, each the other's good-luck harbinger.

Finally, our guide directs us to turn away from the riverbed and up the bank to a narrow footpath. We thrash our way through cacti and branches until, sure enough, we come out on the road to Bassin-Bleu! We tip our guide, and before letting him out, we all insist on shaking his hand.

Now it's a race against time, and yet how much speed

can you pick up on a very bad road? Bill is determined to show us. "Please, honey," I keep pleading with him.

"I'm not going fast." And he's right: sixty kilometers is nothing, under forty miles, if you're on a decent road. The guys in the back are holding on for dear life. "They're not complaining," Bill points out. Of course, they're not going to complain to the guy giving them a free ride home to Haiti.

And so we hurtle toward Bassin-Bleu. At Trois Rivières we make a brief stop to fill up two empty five-gallon bottles with water for washing ourselves. And then the rain starts, a soft, misting rain. A little ways down the path on the other side of the river, we stop to let Wilson off in front of a dilapidated wooden shack.

Next stop, Charlie's, or bust! But every time we clear a hurdle, along comes another one. This is the moment when we meet the young man, carrying a bed frame home to his bride in the rain. How can we not help him? Several kilometers after dropping off man and bed frame, and almost a full hour since we crossed Trois Rivières, we arrive at Charlie's house, cloaked in darkness.

Charlie's family has been on the lookout for us, including little Soliana, sadly parted from her older sister Rica, who is now studying in Gros Morne. (The start of a glorious trend in rural Haiti: young girls getting an education?)

One of Charlie's sisters, Roselin, whom I do not remember from last year, joins the greeting party. She's tall, pretty, and worried-looking. We soon find out why. Her sickly baby is wailing inside the house. He has had diarrhea for days, won't keep anything down. Her four-year-old, Rachel, peers from behind her mother's skirt, mesmerized: white people with suitcases, backpacks, flashlights, digital cameras. Best of all: sack after sack of staples.

We quickly unpack the back of the pickup. Everything has to be carried inside, out of the rain. Piti hurries to help us all get settled, including Eseline, who will be spending the night in Charlie's house with Ludy. It's too dark, on this overcast night, for her to be hiking anywhere with a baby. Once we're ready to sit down and eat, Piti excuses himself from supper. He needs to get going. He has to walk up to his mother's house and then hike over to Eseline's to inform them of our visit tomorrow — a mission of several hours.

Before we bed down, Roselin motions for me to come look at her sickly baby. Jean Kelly lies on a bed in a narrow back room with Rachel bent over him. His sad, dark eyes look huge in his gaunt little face. Maybe because he reminds me of the toddler at Hôpital Sacré Coeur yesterday, I get this awful sense that Jean Kelly is not long for this world. This is what a sixty percent infant mortality rate looks like face-to-face: one anguished mother and her unhappy, feverish baby.

Roselin's worried eyes search mine. A look that assumes I know what can be done to save her baby. What do I tell her? I could point upward like the angry man at the roadblock this afternoon. Only God can help you. Money could also help, if there were a drugstore nearby with medicines she could buy. Little Rachel watches me with curious eyes. Why is the *blan* lady tearing up? This is everyday life in Haiti. There is nothing — and everything — to cry about.

As we are ready to crawl into bed, Charlie's sister, Tanessa, whom I do recall from last year, enters with two bedpans, one for Mikaela, one for us, to put under our beds. No doubt she remembers that one of the guests last summer peed in their front yard. *"Mèsi,"* I say, incriminating myself with an embarrassed smile.

And while we're saying thank you, I remember to tell Bill that he did a great job getting us here safely. Eleven hours on the road, and not one mishap that we could call our fault. One more thing. "You were right about the mango ladies," I finally concede. Why does it take a baby at death's door for me to give up being petty?

All night, on and off, I wake to Jean Kelly's wailing.

Let him make it, I find myself praying. And as if any god worthy to be God would engage in such transactions, I offer to trade him any number of downpours for Jean Kelly's recovery.

July 7, a day (and a night) in the life of Moustique

Infancia's question

Toward morning, the baby stops wailing. But instead of taking this as a good sign and sinking into welcome sleep, I start worrying that something has happened to Jean Kelly. I decide to get up and inquire how he is doing.

Outside, not only is the sun shining, but Roselin is sitting on a cane chair, bouncing Jean Kelly on her lap. His fever has broken! His mother shows him off proudly. He is a beautiful baby.

We hang out in the yard, drinking coffee Bill makes with a *colador,* a cloth sieve he brought from the DR. It occurs to me that we haven't seen any sign of Daddy. When I ask after him, Charlie responds, "He is gone to his home." Maybe because of my worries about Jean Kelly, it occurs to me that Daddy might have died. "Is Daddy okay?"

"Daddy is very okay," Charlie replies.

The word must have gone out that I was asking after him, because a few minutes later, Daddy appears, looking very okay indeed, lean and tall and handsome like his son. But—and I remember this from before—Daddy seems a little lost in this world. He is probably still grieving over his wife, who died two years ago. She must have been a beloved matriarch. At the mention of her name, a pall of sadness descends on all members of the family.

Our first task after breakfast is organizing the supplies we stacked on every available surface last night in the dark. Piti and Eseline sort through the sacks of rice, beans, sugar, oil, making three piles. We thought there would be only two lucky recipients of our gifts: Piti's mother and Eseline's family. (Our arrangement with Charlie is to pay him cash, as we would a hotel.) But how can Piti and Eseline pile up their abundance in front of so many needy faces and not share? The third pile is for Charlie's family. Everyone looks on, smiling.

Midmorning, we drive uphill on the dirt path to Piti's mother's house. "I can't believe you walked all this way last night," I say, shaking my head. Piti grins in reply. I can tell he's often amused by my surprise at what he takes to be just a matter of course.

The path ends, and we climb out of the pickup to walk the rest of the way. Eseline takes the lead. Suddenly, she lets out a cry, and runs off the path, thrashing through the corn-field. It takes the rest of us a moment to spot the tiny woman working in the middle of her patch.

Eseline pulls her mother-in-law by the hand toward the path to meet us. But Piti's mother is holding back, pointing to her dirty dress, her muddy bare feet. Later, she will ex-plain to Piti that she was all set to receive us early this morn-ing. But when we didn't appear, she figured we had changed our plans. Besides, she had work to do.

Well, two mountains cannot meet, but two people can. Bill and I trek into the field to greet her. She grabs each of us in turn, rocking us in her arms, as if we, too, are her chil-dren who have come home.

Mama Piti joins us on the path, drawn by the bait of her little granddaughter asleep in her father's arms. Piti lifts the facecloth draped over Ludy's face to keep the sun from her eyes. Mama Piti has been grinning since we met her, lips pressed together, as if trying to suppress a smile. But now, she lets loose and smiles widely. I see what she's been hiding: her front teeth are missing.

We walk down toward the house, the path too narrow for keeping our arms around each other, though we keep trying. In the hollow sits the small house, the metal roof rusted, the mud walls cracked and crumbling in patches — the house of an old woman whose children have grown up and moved away. In fact, four of her five sons have gone to work in la République. In a plaintive moment, she asks me something that at first Piti is reluctant to translate. "Why have you taken all my sons?"

Mama Piti disappears inside her house. I assume she's getting us some coffee or some chairs to sit on. But as we tour her garden with Piti, we find her in the backyard just finishing up washing her feet and changing into her company outfit: a faded red-and-white print dress with a black belt. Her straw hat is gone, and instead she has donned a fresh kerchief tied around her head.

We stand around for a while—chairs seem scarce here—watching Ludy and her grandmother get acquainted. It's hard to visit when you don't share a language. Piti translates into Kreyòl, then back to Spanish, then to Kreyòl again. At one point, I ask for his mother's name so as not to keep referring to her as Mama Piti. Infancia, a funny name for an old lady, Infancy. As for her age, she is not sure. Maybe she is seventy? Her response is a question, as if her age were up to us to determine.

It occurs to me that in our excitement to get going, we forgot his mother's pile of staples back at Charlie's house! Piti translates for his mother — her gifts are coming later: rice and beans and sugar, cans of tomato paste and sardines, boxes of chocolate and spaghetti. Infancia smiles widely. There have to be some perks to having sons working in la République.

It's closing in on noon, and we still have the longer outing to Eseline's family to deliver her and the baby. Infancia walks us back to the truck. As we say our farewells, I can't help feeling that, while I'm not responsible for all her sons, I am accountable for one of them being gone. I know no way to make it up to Infancia except to promise that I will take care of her son. Piti translates my words. I look in her eyes, trying to say what can't be put into words, even if we did speak the same language.

She gazes back at me. Her eyes are her son's eyes, which I'll get to see much more often than she will.

The great problems of the world

We wolf down lunch — our standard quick meal on this trip: *casave* and cheese, and whatever fruit is on hand — then pile up the gifts in the back. It would be a heavy load to try to carry to Eseline's house. But Piti assures us that Eseline's family has been forewarned and will be waiting for us on the road with their donkey.

We are all feeling excited for Eseline, reuniting with

her family after almost a year away. But also for Charlie, who'll be making a formal petition to Rozla's parents to marry their daughter. I'd be sweating bullets, but Charlie looks his usual unflappable self, in his yellow polo shirt and reflector sunglasses. Although it has been a long time since I was that young, I have to confess that every time I'm around him, I feel like I'm back in high school. Charlie is the kind of totally cool guy who was nice to everyone, but we all knew we were way over our heads in his presence. I don't know what the equivalent is in Moustique, but I can't imagine that Rozla's parents will find fault with him.

Actually, come to think of it, those cool high school studs were precisely the guys our parents did not want us to date. Charlie's coolness could work against him. By Eseline's own admission, her father is not easy. With six daughters, and only one son, Papa keeps a tight rein. Look at the hard time he gave Piti because the poor guy couldn't come up with a pair of earrings! If Eseline's father found fault with Piti, he'll find fault with anybody. Charlie might well be sent packing.

I wish I had the familiarity with Charlie that I have with Piti, so I could give him a little coaching. The reflector glasses should go. The kerchief he likes to tie like an ascot around his neck—it sends the wrong message. The kind of thing that might fly in a resort in the Bahamas, but not with Papa Eseline, who is, after all, a dirt farmer, a man who wore his work clothes to his daughter's wedding.

But I'm not that close to Charlie, and besides, who knows how the marriage brokerage system works here. What asset trumps what flaw. Rozla's parents might well be impressed by Charlie's credentials: his work sojourns in the Bahamas and in the Dominican Republic. His nice house with a concrete foundation and a zinc roof. His little English and Spanish. What I can do is put in my two cents whenever I get the chance. Using my minimal French and my increasingly evolving mime skills, I'll let Eseline's parents know that Charlie *est très bon, très intelligent, très très magnifique.* Haiti has brought out the Yenta in me.

Piti had told his in-laws that we would be at the spot where the path meets the road at noon. But it's past one o'clock by the time we pull over. We're happy to see that the welcome committee has not given up: three of Eseline's sisters and a tiny donkey are waiting for us. Eseline throws open the back door before the pickup has stopped moving and jumps out to greet them. The sisters all hug each other, exclaiming and giggling, like a bunch of cheerleaders. My heart feels as if it has sprouted wings, beating at the doors of my rib cage, wanting to soar above this happy scene. I make the mistake of looking up, only to see thunderclouds moving across the sky toward us. I remember the deal I made last night and shudder.

Once we start unloading the back of the pickup, I'm thinking, no way that poor donkey can carry all this stuff in its two saddlebags. The older of the three waiting sisters, Lanessa, takes charge. She is a tall, slender girl in her teens, the daughter who comes after Rozla. Lanessa begins loading the saddlebags until they are stuffed. The poor donkey grunts under the weight of it all. At moments like this I find myself revisiting the idea of reincarnation. What brutish dictator, or cruel warrior, has come back to pay his dues?

Lanessa finally loops the rope around the top of the load and around the donkey's middle and pulls tight, leaning back on her heels. The donkey rocks as if it is going to fall over. Finally, the load secured, we are on our way, Lanessa leading the donkey, rope in hand, gifts piled high. Her red T-shirt reads SANTA LOVES ME. Today, it seems, he does.

We climb up and down hill, single file on the narrow path, a reminder of last year's journey: the wedding party accompanying the young bride, who was departing for what must have seemed a far-off land. Now we are bringing her back.

As we clear the top of another hill, the donkey starts trotting, and Eseline picks up her steps. Sure enough, there below is her parents' house in the clearing. A bunch of little girls and one lone boy race uphill to meet us. Behind them, an older woman—probably all of forty or younger—throws her arms out in joyous welcome. There are howls of happiness as mother and daughter fall into each other's embrace.

JULIA ALVAREZ

The baby gets handed around. Ludy has got to be what I call a "Buddha baby": taking in all the excitement with a bemused expression. Ho-hum, another day in the human race. She is carried away by three of Eseline's little sisters, who range in age from eight to eleven, still at the stage to be playing with dolls. But the little sisters don't confine themselves to one small doll. They've also taken Mikaela with them, down a path to the other houses that surround this one. "What were they up to?" I ask later when she has been returned.

Mikaela herself isn't sure. "They took me from house to house and showed me to their families. They also wanted to play with my hair." A petite young woman with a head of curls and blue eyes — dolls don't get any prettier.

Later, when asked about my family, I'll pull out a wallet photo of my own two pretty, blonde-haired grand-daughters. Lanessa takes the photo in her two hands, poring over it. She says something to Piti, who translates. "Can she please, please have it to keep?" I feel a little disconcerted. Lanessa doesn't even know who these girls are! But owning their picture is a way of having them, at least to look at. I let her keep it. I have plenty more where that came from.

While the little girls are off playing dolls with Ludy and Mikaela, Bill and I are led by the hand under the awning and sat down on two cane chairs like older dolls ourselves. Piti and Eseline chatter away with her parents, while Bill and I look on, pleased to see them all so happy.

Periodically, Eseline's mother turns to me and utters an exclamation with lifted arms in the manner of a believer at a tent revival. I start to get the feeling I should respond in kind. "We love Piti, we love Eseline, and Ludy — " Loude Sendjika, I have to remember to call her here. And while I'm at it: "We love Charlie. Charlie, *c'est un bon homme.*" Bill flashes me a look. *Hold the gush, before you ruin everything.* Charlie hasn't spoken up yet, and the parents might get upset at a romance begun without their blessing.

Just as with Infancia, it's difficult to visit when you can't carry on a conversation. An activity helps. Luckily, Eseline brings out the wedding album of photos I put together for her. The little girls have rejoined us, clustering around as I turn the pages. They get a kick out of identifying faces in the photos, or looking down shyly when someone points them out, as if there is something embarrassing about being caught by a camera's lens.

After we've gone through the album several times, the girls who were at the periphery of our circle cart it away, to pore over themselves. Perhaps thinking that if one book brought such pleasure, another book will work as well, one of the little sisters brings out Lanessa's school notebook for us to review. Lanessa snatches it, narrowing her eyes at her little sister. "I'd love to look through it," I tell Piti to tell her. I'm curious to see what students are are being taught here in rural Haiti.

Her parents nod sharply at Lanessa to hand over her notebook. What else can they offer their visitors? Lanessa obeys, but then disappears inside the house, as if she is the one now embarrassed to be caught learning.

Seconds later, she peeks coyly out the doorway at me. I smile at her, and hold the notebook to my heart, pantomining that I'd like to look through it. She smiles back. I think that means permission granted.

It is an education to go through the pages of her notebook. Rote learning is alive and well in Moustique. Each entry consists of a question and an answer—a kind of catechism, I take it, of what a young person should know. Lanessa's handwriting is barely legible, and there are many misspellings, which might have originated with whatever text the students were given to copy. The lessons are an odd mix of sex education (A list of the symptoms of AIDS is followed by a list of three ways to prevent getting AIDS in the first place: protect yourself, only one sexual partner, and, a favorite with teens, abstinence); of geography (The "grandes pais dan le mondial," the great countries of the world, are listed as Israel, Great Britain,

Japan, France, Canada, and "l'Allemagne de l''ouest,"
West Germany, which hasn't existed since 1991; a pointed
omission — no United States); and of global politics (The
great problems of the world are: hunger, poverty, pollu-
tion, racism, war, and, finally, erosion. Fair enough. The
ensuing question asks students to "propose a solution for
each one." Not surprisingly, the pages after this last question are blank).

After a good hour of visiting, I'm wondering if the
Charlie conference is ever going to take place. It's closing
on four, and Bill and I already set four-thirty as the hour
of our departure. That will give us enough time to walk
back to the pickup and get to Charlie's before dark. We
don't want a repeat of last night.

Later, I'll realize how astutely Piti managed the tim-
ing of Charlie's petition. Since the wedding, and now with
this return, Piti has become a *gwo nèg*, a big man in the
family. But this is a new role, and Piti has to play his cards
just right with his jealous father-in-law.

Piti nods to Eseline, who goes inside, and comes out
with a plastic bag. Back in the Dominican Republic, Piti
had asked to stop at a farm supply shop for a gift for his
father-in-law: two dozen yards of thick red rope, enough to
tie down any number of loads on any number of donkeys.

The minute Piti pulls it out, Eseline's father leaps up, grabs the rope, grabs Piti, rocking him in an embrace, howling with joy. Together, they measure out the rope, then coil it up in neat loops. More embraces, more exclamations. Sensing the moment has come, Piti murmurs something to his father-in-law, who glances over at Charlie. Then, the three men walk off to a clearing up a slight incline beside the house.

"Just the men," I grouse to Bill, as if it being his gender, he's responsible.

Eseline's mother stays behind, smiling widely, whenever we look at her. She, too, like Infancia, is missing most of her teeth. I'd love to ask her questions, find out her name, how it's been for her this year with her eldest daughter gone. But our translator has more important matters at hand. We can hear his soft-spoken voice wafting down to us. Eseline's father responds with an explosion of words, loud and emphatic. I recall his long peroration at the end of the wedding. He seems an excitable man with strong passions. Look how he went crazy over that rope. Meanwhile, Charlie says not a word.

I don't know if Eseline's mother is growing impatient herself. But fifteen or so minutes into the conference, without warning, she gets up and walks uphill to the gathering.

We exchange a look all around, a look that throws Eseline into a fit of giggles.

I assume that her mother will cut to the chase and the group finally descend with a verdict. But it's a case of sending one messenger after another, and neither one returns. Finally, using the same remedy for impatience as when we waited on the road for the stuck trucks to come unstuck, I invite Mikaela to meditate. Surprisingly, given his dismissal of all things New Agey, Bill asks to join us. By way of explanation to Eseline and her sisters, I put my hands together in prayer and close my eyes. I figure prayer, meditation, what's the difference? Eseline and Piti have asked me on more than one occasion if we are missionaries.

We set up our chairs at the side of the house, facing the incline where the marriage discussion is going on. We meditate for a good twenty minutes — or rather Mikaela and I do. I can hear Bill's soft snores. So that's why he wanted to join us!

Finally, I hear movement and open my eyes. The group is coming down the hill. I lift my eyebrows at Charlie, who returns a small smile. No flashy grin, or thumbs-up cockiness — but then effusiveness would not be Charlie's style. We'll just have to wait until the walk back to the pickup to find out the outcome of his petition.

It's time to go. Eseline's family walk us down the path. When we get to the hilltop where we first spied them, they stop. Piti gathers his baby in his arms, but Ludy is more intrigued with the piece of coconut meat one of her young aunties gave her than in returning a good-bye kiss.

Piti and Eseline's farewell is so matter-of-fact, I'm left wondering if they just can't give themselves the "luxury" of feeling sad. In her essay, "Daughters of Memory," the Haitian-American writer Edwidge Danticat asks, "Is all suffering equal . . . when the people who suffer are not considered equal?" It's an unsettling question that makes me remember this moment in Moustique as well as Piti's occasional bemusement at my surprise that he should have to undergo something I would forgo as too difficult or taxing or painful. You, his look says to me, you have the choice to do otherwise.

Mortal traffic

There's no fooling ourselves, it's raining now. The walk back to the pickup is a no-nonsense trot and not the moment to go into details of the marriage meeting. Briefly, both Piti and Charlie agree it went well. But their very lack of elation leaves me thinking that there must have been some caveats. Maybe the idea of earrings was marched out again? Maybe upped to both a pair of earrings and a couple of rings?

Once we're safely in the pickup, with the rain drumming on the roof, we hear the details. As I thought, there is a caveat. It turns out that there is an even bigger big man in the family than Piti: an uncle who is working in the Bahamas. This uncle is probably the key diaspora relative who sends money back to the family. Charlie must call Rozla's uncle and get his approval before the lovers can proceed.

As we're talking, Charlie pulls out a small, dog-eared photo from his pocket. I'm thinking it's a picture of his beloved Rozla, so it takes me a moment to register the tiny figure in a blue dress engulfed in the satiny interior of a large, white coffin. "My mommy," Charlie explains. It is an odd moment to bring her up.

The photo makes its rounds, all of us responding with respectful silence. What can you say about a picture of somebody's mother in a coffin? Perhaps for Charlie, as for Lanessa with the picture of my pretty granddaughters, having a photo of his deceased mother is a way to have her, if only to look at.

I think of my own parents, and how I still have them, however compromised that having now is. At ninety-five and eighty-five, they are incredibly old, especially by Haitian standards, but even by Dominican ones. Most of their contemporaries have died or are falling fast. It seems every month I get a call: another aunt, uncle, older cousin, fond family friend is gone. The losses keep mounting. The world keeps filling with strangers.

I find myself feeling like that donkey, on a metaphysical level: loaded down with the burden of the mystery, the what's-it-all-about-Alfie feeling that can pull me down into depression for weeks on end. To distract myself, I look out the window, which itself is tearing with raindrops, and what do I see? Three little boys squatting in the rain under an umbrella, flying a kite. Haiti is again talking to me.

"Piti, remember when I first met you?" I ask him.
"You were flying a kite. "He was not much older than the
three boys looking over at us. Now Piti is a man with a
wife and a daughter. This is what life offers as a compensa-
tion for the old ones going out: the young ones coming in.
The mortal traffic can be dizzying, especially when yours
is the next generation on its way out. But as a friend once
told me, after fifty our job is to keep our spirits up, so as not
to scare the ones who are coming after us. The kite dives
but then recovers and soars again. How heavy a rainstorm
will it take to bring it down?

Songlines

By the time we get back to Charlie's, the rain is so loud on the roof of the pickup that we have to shout to hear each other. Inside the house, we exchange one echo chamber for another, with the rain now drumming on the zinc roof.

Tonight, Jean Kelly—for whose recovery I traded this rainstorm—is lively, kicking his little feet, and smiling. Bill thinks the baby probably had some intestinal bug, not uncommon in rural Haiti where potable water is hard to come by. It's why we brought our own, and why we're being especially careful with what we drink and eat. At supper, however, Bill loses his resolve and ventures into a bowl of some stewed meat Charlie's family is chugging down. "What is it?" I ask him. He isn't sure. "And you're going to *eat* it?"

"They eat it," Bill replies, shrugging.

After supper, we decide to turn in early. The rain on the roof is acting like a soporific, that steady hum of a white-noise machine. Charlie's family and Piti wander off to the back room. Suddenly, we hear greetings, laughter, exclamations. Some visitors have arrived at the back door. After some conversation, Piti begins strumming his guitar and singing the hymns that his band used to play up at the farm.

Bill and Mikaela and I peek in at the doorway, hoping to join the impromptu gathering. The visitors turn out to be Piti's oldest sister and her husband, as well as Infancia, who has come to collect her gifts. In a heavy rainstorm? More likely, Piti's mother was missing him, and this is one last opportunity to see him before he departs with us at dawn.

We all pile on the one bed, singing along as Piti plays hymn after hymn. Then—I don't know what propels us—but Infancia and I both get up and begin dancing to-gether, while the others look on. There's life in the two old women yet!

Soliana and Tanessa are the first to break into the circle, then Mikaela. Soon all the females in the room have joined hands, and we are dancing on whatever available floor space we can find. The men sing to us, celebrating the female generations, from Rachel to Infancia, sunrise to sunset.

When the song is over, we pile onto the bed and cede the floor to the men: Charlie; and Tanessa's husband, Jimmy; and Daddy, who must have heard us singing and crossed over to the party. Piti keeps playing his guitar, the women singing, the men holding hands and dancing. Something is in the air, we can feel it, humming inside us, outside us, as the rain keeps coming down.

Later in bed, Bill whispers in my ear, "Wow, that was . . . something."

I, too, don't know what to call what happened that night in Moustique. The Australian Aborigines believe there are invisible songlines holding the world together, lines that have to be sung afresh with each generation to keep the land and the people alive. That night in Moustique, we were singing and dancing them. Just shy of six months after the earthquake, we were putting Haiti back together again, however briefly, in our imaginations.

July 8 — On the road to Port-au-Prince

An earthquake, a flood, a river gang, a fight

I n the middle of the night, I wake up to a high-pitched humming. Next thing I know the roof of the small house is flapping like a loose wing that might fly off. I think of waking Bill. But just as suddenly as it came, whatever it was is gone.

We wake up early to a glorious, sunny morning. Outside, everyone is talking about the tremor last night. So that's what it was: an earthquake! It seems these slight tremors are common, but now people can't help wondering if, this time, the tremor will turn into a real earthquake.

We eat a hurried breakfast, eager to get on the road and face whatever we're going to have to face. This time around, packing the pickup is quick and easy, as our load is gone. Mikaela, Bill, Piti, and I climb in and wave back to our hosts, who have come down to the road to say good-bye.

We haven't gone far when we begin to experience the results of yesterday's heavy rains. The road to the river is a mud slick, with water running in deepened ruts on either side. Bill is finding it hard to steer, as the pickup doesn't have mud tires. At one point, he slides into a thick hedge of bayonet cacti, which luckily catches us and prevents us from plunging off the road and into a ditch. But as he puts the pickup in reverse, trying to extricate himself from the net of thorny branches, there's a horrible tearing sound.

Bill gets out to inspect damage, and I can tell it's not good news. It turns out the front fender has snapped loose, and the sideview mirror is bent at a weird angle. This is Bill's relatively new pickup, which he debated buying, as he's not a guy to get the latest model if the old one still works. I stop myself from trying to comfort him. ("Now you don't have to worry about that first dent.") I know how annoying comfort can be when all you want to do is vent.

With Piti's help, Bill somehow manages to manipulate the mirror and the fender back in place — though periodically the fender swings loose, and we have to stop and secure it again.

We're back on the road, holding our breaths whenever we come to a particularly muddy patch. I can see now that we should have waited to set out until later in the day when the mud would have had a chance to dry and harden. Another thing I shouldn't bring up. But this time my nerves get the better of me. I try to mitigate the insult of suggesting an alternative by addressing my question to Piti in Spanish.

"What do you think, Piti?" I ask him. "Should we wait awhile?" We could just stop right here, hold an extended meditation session inside the pickup, while Bill naps.

"I am not worried about the road," Piti replies, but before I can feel reassured, he adds, "What worries me is the river."

It is amazing that, with my overactive imagination, I have not yet worked out what happens when a heavy rainstorm swells a river, actually a confluence of three rivers. But I make up for my oversight now by imagining the worst-case scenario: all of us carried away by the current, in a big, dented, silver casket. And nobody to take our picture.

"Piti says the river will be high," I translate for Bill. No response. I'm about to repeat myself on the unlikely chance that he didn't hear me. But as we round the last bend, there is no need to. Before us lies the river, a big, bloated beast. Piti's intake of breath is audible. On the far bank, people have gathered, waiting for the river to go down before crossing.

Just as he must not have heard me, Bill must not have seen the river, because when he gets to the edge, he steps on the gas.

"What are you doing?" I scream as we lunge into the water. "Are you crazy?" What a time to ask!

"Calm down," he snaps. "It's shallow here."

Mikaela and Piti are silent in the backseat. Who can blame them? I'm the one who's crazy, fighting with a madman who has our lives in his hands.

We do make it through the shallows to a sandbar. To his credit, Bill is sane enough to stop, disembark, and assess the situation. We look out at the wider, deeper part of the river, swirling in currents, running swiftly downstream.

JULIA ALVAREZ

A crowd of young men who had been waiting at the far shore wade over to the sandbar. Each one is shouting some suggestion.

"Just ignore them," Bill orders, like it's that easy to ignore someone shouting in your face.

Piti confers with one of the quieter young men. It seems there is no other spot, upstream or downstream, suitable for crossing. "We can make it," Bill keeps saying. But Piti insists on checking it out first. He strips down to his underwear and wades across the river, disappearing up to his shoulders, before his body reemerges on the other side. Not good news. He comes back and advises that really we should wait.

"Okay, twenty minutes," Bill reluctantly agrees.

"Nothing is going to happen in twenty minutes." I try to reason with him. "Come on, honey, it's not even eight thirty."

Bill looks at his watch. Unfortunately, several Christmases ago, I got him one of those atomic watches that sets itself via satellite, so Bill can never be wrong about what time it is. "It's eight forty-three. And I'm not waiting more than twenty minutes."

"Well I am. And so is Piti, and so is Mikaela." What's he going to do: leave the three of us stranded on a sandbar in northwest Haiti? "Honey, come on, please," I try the gentle approach. "Why don't we use the time to talk?"

"We can talk on the way to Port-au-Prince." Then after a beat, "What do you want to talk about anyway?"

I'm trying to come up with an answer when I'm saved by the approach of a familiar figure, joining us on the sandbar. Wilson! He was headed to Bassin-Bleu to visit some relations. But now, he delays his journey to help us out. What did I say about saving by spending? We did a good turn by taking him home to Haiti. Now he is ready to pay us back by helping us get across the river, so we can eventually get home to the DR.

Wilson strips down to his underwear and gives Mikaela and me his dry clothes to hold in the cab. He and

Piti wade into the waters to map out the shallowest route for the pickup to cross. Bill stands on the shore, periodically shouting suggestions.

Meanwhile, the river gang have grown bored watching them work. They crowd around the opened windows of the pickup where Mikaela and I are sitting, blocking all ventilation. We decide to climb out, in part to get some air, but also to move the guys away from the cab. They've been checking it out, looking for some loose valuable or small trinket they can snatch or demand as payment for their help.

As we're standing around, one of them suddenly grabs at the water bottle Mikaela is holding. I face down the would-be petty thief, hands on my hips. *"C'est ma fille,"* I roar. "That's my daughter." I've turned into the lioness whose cub has just been messed with. And I'm accusing Bill of trying to get us all killed! This guy might be skinny, but he is several inches taller and at least thirty pounds heavier than I am. Interestingly, the other guys turn on this young man and shove him away. He's broken some basic code of honor they all follow. You don't mess with a girl in the presence of her mother.

But soon they're back to hollering suggestions, pointing to the other side. A few of them pick up some stones from the sandbar, carry them across the river, and lay them down on the other bank. Are they planning to build a bridge? I shake my head and keep repeating, "Patience, patience," just like the many *banques* in their country advise. Then, partly to show off, and partly to entertain them, Mikaela and I strike a yoga tree pose. A few of them try imitating us.

Another vehicle now comes barreling through the shallows and joins us on the sandbar. It's a Jeep with a CARE logo on the side. Mikaela and I rush over, thinking it might be driven by someone who speaks English. No luck. The driver, a light-skinned Haitian, looks us both over. I can almost hear his thinking: Why are you two white women doing exercises on this sandbar? Over our shoulders, Bill is gesticulating to Piti and Wilson, who are midstream, gesticulating back. That must answer the driver's question, because he nods at us, puts his foot to the pedal, and hurtles across the river, and up the other bank. This seals our fate. Bill has been proven right: if the Jeep made it, so will our pickup.

Bill hurries over to where Mikaela and I have resumed our tree poses. "Okay," he says, "we're off." Piti and Wilson are already standing at different points in the river, semaphoring directions. But the river gang is not about to let us go. They press in on us, demanding payment.

Bill tells me to tell them that they must stay away from the truck. Once we're in the water, he won't be able to see where they are. They might trip or fall, and the truck could run them over.

I try my best to mime this homicide scenario, ending with putting my hands together in the gesture of pleading. They look at each other, as if deciding whether to obey the white man's instructions. Okay, they nod. This might be their only chance of getting the tip they obviously feel they deserve.

"Everything off the floor in case the cab floods," Bill commands, as he starts the engine. Oh dear. He would have to say that.

"How about our seat belts?" I ask, terrified.

"I wouldn't," Bill answers. I suppose that means I shouldn't, either. "Okay, here we go!" As the pickup lunges forward, two small hands reach forward from the back-seat for my hands. I take them and squeeze. "Say a little prayer!" I call back to Mikaela. I know from several of our talks about religion that Mikaela is a practicing Catholic, the radical liberation theology strain of Catholicism of her activist parents. As a child, Mikaela would be taken along to demonstrations as well as open-air services in public parks. Half the time, she didn't know if she was attending a mass or a mass rally. She is the only one in this cab whose prayer God would not dismiss with the remark, "*Now* you come to me!"

We splash our way across the river and roar up the bank over the few rocks the guys have laid down. Mikaela and I cheer. But our elation is short-lived. The river gang have come racing across the river and up the bank, claiming credit for what just happened and demanding payment.

Piti and Wilson join us. As they climb into their dry clothes, we confer on what to do about the river gang. Part of the problem is that we have run out of cash. Unless we can break down a hundred dollar bill or use a credit card, all we have among us is two hundred pesos.

Soft-spoken Piti is trying to calm the angry mob. But Bill is inciting them more by shaking his head. He is not paying anyone a tip except for the quiet guy who advised Piti. At one point I glance out my window and see a woman, who wasn't even one of the river gang, holding up a rock and menacing me with it.

"You're making things worse," I hiss at Bill.

The crowd quiets down when they see Bill handing Piti some bills to give to the one guy. Bill explains to Piti that as soon as he hands over the money, Piti is to jump in the back of the pickup, and we'll take off. But before

Piti can even take a few steps, the crowd closes in around him. I can't see him at all! These guys are so desperate, they're liable to hurt Piti for a pitiful two hundred pesos, the equivalent of six bucks.

I step out of the pickup, another lioness with her cub moment. But just then, Piti disentangles himself from the mob and runs toward the truck. "Get in!" Bill screams to me. I don't even think about disagreeing. I jump in, bang the door shut, just as Piti clambers on board, and we roar off, down the road. A few guys start to run after us, but finally give up.

When we're well down the road, beyond sight, we stop so Piti and Wilson can come inside the cab. "They almost tore off my hand," Piti recounts, still trying to catch his breath, his eyes wide with fear. The money never got to the guy who had helped us out.

"We should go back." I know it's a foolish suggestion, and a cowardly one: putting others in the position of being the tough-hearted ones, having to naysay my easy kindness.

We're all sobered by this scary moment. And what's even scarier is that this might well be the story of the future, with far more violent conclusions, unless we begin to solve one of the great problems in the world: the inequitable distribution of goods. Here, six months after the earthquake, with millions of dollars pledged and a cadre of well-meaning people on the ground, solutions to this problem continue to evade even the best efforts. Those pages are still a blank in so many of our notebooks.

To Port-au-Prince or not?

We let Wilson off in Bassin-Bleu, and then begins the heated debate: whether or not to proceed to Port-au-Prince or go back the way we came, over roads we know. Actually, Piti and Mikaela are silent in the back-seat. It's Bill and me at odds about what to do next.

It's not that I am chickening out on our earlier plans. It's that I feel shaken by what just happened. We have no idea what the roads to Port-au-Prince will be like. What if there are more swollen rivers, more mob scenes? I want us to think through each choice and make an informed decision.

Bill makes a face. "I've thought it through," he says.

"I know you've thought it through, but I'm talking about thinking it through together."

"Okay, let's think it through together. I think we should go. What do you think?"

Am I really married to this bloke? If two sweet young people weren't sitting in the backseat, I'd give this guy a mouthful. Instead I seethe. "That's not thinking it through together. That's making a decision before we even start."

I turn around to the backseat. "I'm sorry you have to listen to this."

Mikaela giggles. "Don't worry about it. I've traveled with my family." I guess it is a universal truth: families, especially spouses, bicker on road trips.

Piti has the soul of a peacemaker, but he also has a male bias, as we saw by his chauvinist remark the night before his own wedding. Now he points out that we've passed several packed buses coming from the capital. If the roads were impassable, they would not have gotten through.

"But are you sure that's where they're coming from?"

"Yes. There are seven of them a day; we have passed five already." He has been counting them.

That is the kind of reasoning I was hoping for. The fear of impassable roads is laid to rest. The other fear is just that, a fear, not a reason to cancel the trip. I can acknowledge it to myself, though not out loud to a partner I'm at odds with. And this is it: after witnessing the desperation of people in a place where there hasn't even been a horrible natural disaster, I am worried about what we will encounter in a place where people have every reason to be desperate.

"So, are we going or not?" Bill has pulled over.

I look out the window, too upset to answer right off. We are parked in front of SOLUTION GARAGE, down the street from EASY GO HOTEL. Haiti isn't just talking to me. She's shouting at me: Be a grown-up! "Yes, we are going to do what you want." I pronounce the words distinctly, as if each one were packed in bubble wrap and would explode if it came in contact with another.

And so, once again, fearsome Eichner wins out over fearful Alvarez. But it's not an easy truce. All the way to Port-au-Prince, our silence is palpable, our conversation so clearly directed at the backseat. Will this keep happening as we grow older, I wonder? As our work lives drop away, and we're thrown together more, will we discover that while we did fine as two parallel solitudes, we do less well as one perfect union? Some marriages function well at certain stages and then go awry — look at Homero's.

Makes me despair that Bill and I can be happy forever after together.

It's at this point that I see the woman wearing the T-shirt that reads, STOP BITCHING: START A REVOLUTION. Maybe I'll do just that. Give it all up and come to Haiti. But as the passing tap-taps keep reminding me (JESUS IS MY LIFE, DIEU SEUL MAÎTRE, AMOUR ET DISCIPLINE, FIDÉLITÉ DIEU), I am hardly a candidate for total self-sacrifice. If the speaking landscape has anything to say about it, Haiti will not take me.

Human GPS

The road south is definitely better than any we've been on before. But I'm distracted by the emotions roiling inside me.

Past Saint-Marc, about halfway to Port-au-Prince, we look up, and for a moment, we don't understand what we are seeing. The hillsides are speckled with a sickly, plasticky blue—not the beautiful, dreamy blue of shutters and doors in Moustique. Slowly, it dawns on us: these are tarps, held up by sticks. This far out from the capital, the tent cities have started.

As we near Port-au-Prince, we're stuck in one bottle-neck after another. Traffic in the capital has always been a challenge, and now even more so, with many streets blocked by piles of debris, or by trucks carting it away, or by swarms of people who have nowhere else to go. We don't dare leave the main road, as we're not sure that the side streets go where they're supposed to anymore.

Luckily, we have a number to call and a destination. Right before leaving Vermont, a good friend and founder of an international consulting firm sent us the contact infor-mation of the man who has been running the firm's proj-ects in Haiti. Louis is an American, about our age, who has lived in Port-au-Prince for a number of years, speaks Kreyòl, has a Haitian companion — I think that's the way

Elsie is referred to. We should get in touch with him. We thanked our friend, but didn't make much of an effort, focused as we were on getting our paperwork in order with José Ortiz. But we did send a quick e-mail to Louis, and he replied.

Unfortunately, the very week we are in Haiti, Louis and Elsie will be in the Dominican Republic getting some much needed R & R. But Louis gives us the phone number of his son, Adam, who is now in Port-au-Prince, working for the OAS.

Louis also obliges Bill's request to make us a reservation at the Hotel Oloffson for our night in the capital. Bill has been wanting to stay there ever since he had lunch at its terrace restaurant during a brief visit to Haiti in 1983. The hotel, a huge white gingerbread house was immortalized in Graham Greene's novel about Duvalier's Haiti, *The Comedians*, which was set in a fictional version of the Oloffson: a hangout for entrepreneurs, bohemian journalists, CIA cronies hobnobbing with Haitian politicans, Haitian artists and intelligentsia coming up for air. A place where one could count on lots of intrigue and beautiful women and booze.

Making a reservation proves to be more of an ordeal than we realize. Louis actually has to send his driver over to the hotel to secure two rooms for us. Phones are still unreliable, as I know from trying to call the hotel from Vermont. Louis does warn us that the night we plan to stay at the Oloffson, a Thursday, is the night that RAM plays till all hours of the night. I recognize the name of the band that was started by the current Haitian-American proprietor of the hotel, Richard Morse. It's quite loud, Louis adds. Back in Vermont, the warning didn't faze me.

We are able to return the favor and help Louis and Elsie with their accommodations in the Dominican Republic. After spending a day in the capital, they plan to head for the interior. Can we recommend a place to stay? As a matter of fact, we can. How would they like to stay on a coffee farm? A coffee farm? Why . . . sure! And so, just as we are arriving in Port-au-Prince, Elsie and Louis are settling in at Alta Gracia.

As we hit the outskirts, I call Adam for help getting downtown to the Oloffson. After brief greetings, he suggests that we come instead to Pétionville, where his office is and where he lives. From there, he can lead us through the thicket of streets into the center of Port-au-Prince. He gives us a set of directions, using landmarks, not street signage, always in short supply here, and now even more so. We're to call him in twenty minutes, and tell him where we are. Our human GPS! I start doubting that Adam could be from the USA, as such lavish generosity with time most often abounds in less wealthy countries.

Finally, we are in Pétionville, the elite neighborhood in the hills above the poorer Port-au-Prince. It still has an air of prosperity, but it's as if the dividers have been lifted. We pass piles of rubble, devastated buildings, a tent city in a vacant lot, right alongside high-end boutiques, trendy galleries, expensive restaurants.

The Planet Café is in ruins; its sign advertising "multi-services" sits atop slabs of concrete. Were the drivers of the two cars, whose fenders stick out of the rubble, availing themselves of those services when the earthquake struck?

In a vacant lot down the street, another car has been released from the surrounding rubble. Dented, its hood up, it doesn't look like it's going anywhere. I'm puzzled by the flowered sheet curtaining a back window, until a door opens and a man climbs out. This is a family's house.

Some electric poles are still standing, their wires entangled with dozens of small, homemade kites. I'm wondering about the children who lost them. Are they still alive?

As we start climbing uphill, a white pickup with a UN logo pulls up alongside us. Three soldiers in camouflage are standing in the flatbed. They are remarkably handsome in their dark sunglasses and nicely fitting uniforms, like actors in a movie about the earthquake. They grin over at us, and one of them gives us a thumbs-up gesture. He must have spotted Mikaela.

Rather than risk our getting lost one more time, trying to locate his office, Adam directs us to wait outside a restaurant called Papaye on the street we are already on. We pull up on the sidewalk and look around. Papaye looks untouched by the earthquake, except for a missing *e* at the end of the letters bolted on the outside wall.

After hours on the road, Mikaela and I need to use the facilities. Will they let us? we wonder. Two scruffy-looking ladies. It's worth a try.

We walk in, and this will be one of the biggest shocks of all: the huge stretch between the destroyed city, the flimsy tarps, the masses of displaced people, and this plush, soft-lit series of dining alcoves complete with white linen tablecloths and twinkling wine goblets. We might have wandered into a trendy restaurant in Paris or San Francisco. It is a lovely, enticing spot, but given what surrounds it, we feel compromised even using the bathroom. But use it we do, and then hurry out to report on what we found inside.

When Adam pulls up with his driver, I'm surprised. Adam grew up in Vermont, so I was expecting a pale farmboy with blue eyes. Instead he looks Haitian, like one of the light-skinned young men we've been seeing driving up and down the street in their SUVs. Later, we'll learn more of his story. His father, Louis, was in the Peace Corps in the seventies in Niger, where he married a Tuareg woman, Adam's mother. The marriage did not last, and Adam ended up being raised by his dad in the States, so he both is and isn't a typical young American of the under-thirty generation.

Introductions are brief, with effusive thanks on our side. We jump in the pickup and follow Adam's car toward the center of Port-au-Prince. Because it has gotten dark, we are spared the full impact of the devastated city. But we can smell it: sewage and cooking fires and the concrete—sawdust—ground dust smells of construction sites, or more appropriately here, destruction sites. Slowly, figures emerge from the darkness, clusters in front of tarps and tents, women around small fires, basins of water, groupings on the streets, at corners—masses of humanity surviving.

Two more comedians at the Oloffson

Pulling into the Oloffson is another unreal moment. The lobby is lit up and crowded with another kind of humanity, the thriving kind. Little groupings of people I imagine to be journalists sit at tables, talking on cell phones, laptops open. Many are foreign-looking — i.e., white. (Interestingly, the word in Kreyòl for foreigner, *blan*, also means white.) There are plenty of Haitians here, as well, all shades of brown, as this is one of the permeable places in the city where outsiders can come in contact with insiders, those who know or who pretend to know.

As we walk through the restaurant area to the front desk, we spot some members of the band already setting up at the far end of the veranda, testing the sound system. One musician strums a guitar, and the sound from the humongous speakers makes the floor vibrate. How can people traumatized by a recent earthquake not freak out?

At the front desk, the receptionist pages through her guestbook and announces that there is no reservation in our name. Adam steps forward and, with a few words of Kreyòl, resolves the matter. There are only two rooms left. They are going fast. It turns out that the six-month anniversary of the earthquake is in a few days, and the city is flooding with journalists returning to report on how the reconstruction is going. Haiti is again newsworthy.

Bill is ready to hand over his credit card. But Adam suggests we take a look at the rooms first.

We trudge upstairs behind the young porter, leaving Piti in the lobby to guard our belongings. The first room is down a long open-air corridor. It's actually quite pleasant with a big ceiling fan, a magisterial bed, a freestanding floor mirror, and slatted jalousie doors that open onto a balcony that looks down at the garden below. But just as we're about to give our approval, the explosive sounds of electric guitars and drums comes booming through the floor. It turns out the band plays *directly* below this room. No wonder that, in a city filling with journalists, this room is vacant. And RAM regularly plays until three in the morning.

I shake my head at the porter. This will not do.

Almost as if we are connected by a push-pull mechanism, Bill insists we stay. The noise won't be that bad. "We can close all the windows." Great! We'll stay awake all night having a sauna instead.

But it's not just the heat. Even a closed room can't stop the walls and floor from shaking. With scenes of the televised earthquake still fresh in my head, I know I'll be awake all night, thinking it's happening again. "Didn't you just hear that? Didn't you just feel that?"

But Bill claims he didn't hear or feel anything. I'm tempted to turn to Adam and Mikaela and ask for their testimony. But I'm already ashamed enough to be arguing in front of them and the waiting porter.

Two adults should be able to figure this out reasonably. "Let's go outside in the hall and talk about it a second. Will you excuse us?" But out in the hall, Bill isn't any more reasonable. He wants to stay at the Oloffson. He has always wanted to stay at the Oloffson ever since he had lunch in the dining room twenty-seven years ago.

"But don't you want to get some sleep?"

"Okay, OKAY, you win!"

I take a deep breath. I've had enough of this vaudeville act. Then and there, I decide. We are staying at the Oloffson. Mikaela and Adam are at the door. "I'm sorry," I tell them. "I guess we're going to take it."

Into this impasse steps Adam. He reminds us of something that his father had mentioned. Louis, Elsie, and Adam are actually renting two apartments at their compound: one for their use, another to accommodate guests or visiting coworkers. The extra apartment is currently empty; we are more than welcome to stay there. Adam assures us that it's not an imposition on him. We should think of it as a house swap. His father and Elsie are staying at Alta Gracia. It's only fitting that we stay in their guest apartment.

"It's up to Bill," I say, knowing if I agree to anything, there's a good chance he will oppose it.

"Just as long as we can have lunch here," he concedes grumpily.

We descend the stairs and stop at the front desk to let the receptionist know that we won't be taking the rooms, after all. In front of us, a guest with a British accent is explaining that he is checking out for the night so he can get some sleep. He turns, shaking his head. "I adooore Richard," he announces, elongating the middle vowel as only a Brit can do. "But this band idea is a ghastly mistake."

This is so perfect, it saves me a dozen I-told-you-so's.

And so, once again, we follow Adam through the twists and turns of downtown Port-au-Prince and back up to Pétionville. In the Graham Greene novel, the comedians of the title are the white charlatans, so caught up in their personal dramas, they seem oblivious to the deadly despotic regime around them. Even though we didn't end up staying there, Bill and I would fit right in with the other comedians in Greene's version of the Oloffson.

Money to be made among the ruins

Adam pulls up in front of an electric gate that opens; we follow him past several buildings to a cul-de-sac parking area in the rear. The compound was built by a well-off Haitian family for themselves to live in, but they are now using only one of the buildings and are renting out the others. With rents in Port-au-Prince now rivaling those of New York City and LA, the family is cashing in on the demand. We drive past building after building. It's astonishing to think that a single family once lived here, albiet an extended one.

Adam and his father and Elsie are living in a rear building on the top floor above their ground-floor guest apartment. It feels palatial with a living room that opens onto a back terrace, a kitchen, and two bedrooms each with a bath. Piti assures us he won't mind sleeping on the couch. He now confesses that he is very glad we did not stay at the Oloffson. I recall the meek, big-eyed look on his face as he waited in a corner of the lobby with our suit-cases, a young man feeling humbled—by what? I'm curi-ous. What didn't he like about the Oloffson?

Piti shrugs. He just did not feel welcome there. While he was waiting for us, the receptionist, the porters, the people milling around did not look on him kindly.

I'm surprised, as Richard Morse and his band are known for being huge advocates of the Haitian little guy. All I can figure is that Piti hasn't traveled widely in his own country. He has never had much contact with Haitians of the upper class. He has met plenty of upper-class Dominicans in the DR, but perhaps he takes it as a matter of course that he will be second-class in somebody else's country. Among his own people, it stings to feel those differences.

We invite Adam to join us for supper at any place he recommends. He picks a restaurant called Quartier Latin, where a Cuban group plays on Thursday nights. (Thursday nights seem to be music nights in Port-au-Prince.) As we follow Adam's car, we turn and find ourselves engulfed in a crowd that closes around us. There's some sort of open-air concert going on in front of one of the tent cities. People have taken over the street, dancing, singing, waving their arms. Faces peer in at us; hands bang on the pickup in the rhythm of the drums, but also in impatience because we're breaking up their party in order to get through. Ahead of us, Adam has slowed to make sure we are behind him.

My heart is beating as loudly as the drums outside. We are inside the very scene I envisioned this morning when I was tempted to cancel the Port-au-Prince trip, surrounded by people who have every reason to feel desperate.

But nothing happens. We don't get pulled out of our

pickup and told to surrender our wallets at knifepoint. It could be market day at the border in Dajabón, sans the military escort. I am left puzzled by my own expectations. What scenarios have I absorbed from the media or books — the violent history of Haiti can make for nightmare reading — that have led me to assume that poverty and misfortune will always bring out the worst in people?

At the Quartier Latin, we are turned away by the guards at the gate. The place is packed, filled to capacity. The city must be crawling with people who have money to spend. Later, Adam will tell us that there are ten thousand NGOs on the ground — that's not counting the personnel who work for them; seven thousand Brazilian soldiers here with the United Nations; aid workers, journalists, consultants, embassy people. There is money to be made among the ruins, services to be provided for foreigners, many of whom are well-meaning, but also accustomed to a certain level of comfort, of safety, of good food, dependable Internet, fun and entertainment.

We stand on the sidewalk outside Quartier Latin, debating what to do. It's well past nine o'clock. If it were up to me, I'd head back to the compound, open one of our cans of vegetables, another of chickpeas, assuage our hunger, and then crash. But I'm also determined to end this night on a grace note if it kills me. Briefly, I consider injecting some humor in the situation by suggesting we head back to the Oloffson, have dinner there, then dance to RAM till the cows come home.

Adam comes up with an alternate plan. There's a Lebanese-Haitian restaurant he thinks we'll like called Magdoos. It's a short drive to the pull-in parking, across the street from another tent city. Entering through the tall, guarded gates is another unreal moment—like entering Papaye earlier today. But since Bill and Piti didn't have that experience, this place is more of a shock to them. The chandeliers, the crystal, the crimson canopies draping outdoor tables. The place is full of foreigners, embassy people, NGO workers, consultants—most of whom will be gone by the time we are done with our meal. It turns out there is a midnight curfew imposed by many international organizations on their personnel. A safety precaution, Adam explains. This is, after all, a city under siege—by the aftermath of a natural disaster as well as the ongoing onslaught of poverty.

In fact, the United Nations forces have blocked out the city into zones, reminiscent of Baghdad; there is a downtown red zone where foreigners are advised not to go; a more residential yellow zone, where folks are urged to be cautious; and finally a green zone (where we are now, in the hills of Pétionville), a place with no history of trouble.

And yet, the first kidnapping of foreign nationals after the earthquake, back in March, happened right here in Pétionville.

"There are no 'safe' areas in Haiti," the US State Department travel advisory warns on its Web site. It goes on to recommend against nonessential travel. Don't go to Port-au-Prince unless you have to. Which is exactly the opposite of the choice we made this morning, coming here without having to. And I'm glad we did. Yes, I will say it, even to a spouse I'm at odds with. We should be held accountable for our fears, be forced to journey to the hearts of darkness of our own imaginings. We might find ourselves surprised, uttering not "The horror! The horror!" with Joseph Conrad, but "The Beauty! The Beauty!" with Junot Díaz.

We are in luck: a table has just opened. The waiter escorts us to an outside patio and hands us each a large menu like a choir's music folder. I have a brief, absurd image of all of us standing up to sing the Hallelujah chorus.

I'm at one end of the table with Piti, who is gazing down at his menu as if it were written in a foreign language. It might be that he doesn't read French, or perhaps he is shocked at the prices — most entrées are in the mid- to high-twenty-dollar range. With my translation help, he decides on the fried fish, perhaps thinking of Eseline's choice of fish last year in Cap-Haïtien.

At the other end of the table, Bill and Mikaela and Adam are talking about Haiti, the frustrations of the reconstruction, the six-month anniversary on Monday. I'm relieved not to have to participate, as I'm feeling that I can't trust any of my reactions or instincts right now. Only one impulse feels trustworthy: seeing to it that Piti isn't again left out in the cold as he was in the lobby of the Oloffson.

"What a difference from last night!" I say, recalling our singing and dancing in the tiny back room in Moustique.

Piti shakes his head, as if he, too, doesn't believe we got here from there.

"What do you think so far, I mean, about Port-au-Prince?"

Piti's expression is suddenly grave, his forehead lined. It's that old man who occasionally makes an appearance on his baby face, a preview of what he will look like when he is my age. "Poor Haiti needs so much help," he says, sighing. "If I had money, I would help." I wonder if he knows that the majority of people dining at Magdoos tonight came to Haiti with the same idea: to help.

We finish our meal with a half hour to spare before the midnight curfew. On the way back to the compound, Adam takes us on a dry run to the Dominican consulate, so we will be able to find it on our own tomorrow. As we say our goodnights to him, then to Piti and Mikaela, I brace myself. This will be my first time alone with Bill since our full day of squabbling. At dinner, he was chatting away, effusive and happy at last to be among friends, eating good food, anticipating a good night's rest. See, I wanted to call down the table, see what comes of not staying at the Oloffson!

But neither of us has energy for recriminations or I-told-you-so's. What's more, Bill's intrepid eating of the mystery meat dish in Moustique last night has resulted in upset bowels. He admits that he hasn't felt himself all day. "Do you mind if I use the bathroom?" I shake my head, feeling myself melting already at the thought of this bloke, whom I was going to leave forever, dying on me from food poisoning. "I have Pepto-Bismol in my case by the sink if you need it."

The door of the bathroom closes. I sit on the edge of the bed and take a deep breath. I would meditate if I thought it would help. But what's the use? No matter what, I keep coming back to this faulty default self. When Bill finally returns and climbs in beside me I curl into the curve of his body and listen to his breathing a long while, before I, too, fall asleep.

July 9, Port-au-Prince — we came to see

Breakfast at pâtisserie Marie Beliard

The sun is shining brightly through the picture window — so soon after I fell asleep! As I'm coming awake, I hear a soft strumming through the closed door. It's Piti, playing his guitar. He brought it along to Haiti with the idea of leaving it behind for that future day when he will come home to stay. But once in Moustique, he changed his mind. He will need his guitar to make it through the long, lonely months without Eseline and the baby. Right now, hearing him play, I wonder if he needs it just to get through the day, bracing himself for more of what we saw yesterday.

We're eager to get going, figuring we'll find a place open for breakfast. Adam drops in to say good-bye and tells us that there is actually a very good pâtisserie called Marie Beliard on the way to the consulate. "On the way" is one of those slippery phrases I've learned not to trust in Haiti. But Adam, who has not failed us so far — it wasn't his fault the Quartier Latin was packed last night — is right again. We make one left turn on the way to the consulate, and go down about a block, and there it is, a shop with large picture windows and a pull-in parking area not piled high with rubble.

It is breakfast time and the place is hopping. We stand around, trying to figure out the system for ordering. A bemused woman in her forties offers to help in a slightly French-accented English. She reminds me of women I've seen in delicatessens in Manhattan's Upper East Side, so neatly attired — their pumps match their purses — you'd be surprised to learn that all they're dressed up for is this outing.

Madame explains that we must pick a number from a dispenser at the end of the counter; wait for it to pop up on a panel; then we must place our order with our attendant, who writes it up and hands the slip to us; whereupon, we must join that other pressing crowd at the register; pay for our order; get our slip stamped; then return to the first crowd, where we must try to catch the attention of our attendant; hand over our stamped slip; and wait for her to fill our order. I'm exhausted just hearing how to do it.

But the system seems to be working: people keep getting their bags and boxes and going out the door, our patrician lady among them. Meanwhile we wait and wait and wait. Even people whose numbers were after ours have come and gone. Nine o'clock ticks by; we've been waiting over a half hour! I go out to give Piti, not really a progress report, more like a regress report.

Back inside, another English-speaker, a man named

Junior, hears us grumbling and asks what's the problem. When we explain, he puts in a good word for us with one of the attendants, then begins telling us his story. It turns out he lives in Miami with his wife and kids, but he travels back and forth because he has business in Haiti. What kind of business? "I make ice and sell it to restaurants, hotels, grocery stores."

My next question is one that I'm sure everyone in Port-au-Prince must be asked: "Were you here when the earthquake happened?"

Junior's face clouds. He nods slowly. Yes, he was. "The land became the sea." He sways as if reliving the moment. He managed to escape. But it was crazy, crazy: the streets full of frantic people, the dust, the cries. As he talks, the crowd around us grows quiet. Even though Junior is speaking in English, people know that he is talking about *goudou goudou*, the onomatopoeic name that Haitians have given the earthquake, imitating the sound of the ground shaking, the buildings crumbling.

Junior must assume we're missionaries or aid workers, because as he is leaving, he thanks us for coming to Haiti.

I feel embarrassed to be getting credit for something we're not doing. By the same token, it seems coldhearted and not totally accurate to say we didn't come here to help. "We just came to see," I explain.

He looks me in the eye, and I'm bracing myself for a moral scolding. But what he says surprises me, "Haiti needs for people to see it."

"It's like our 9/11," Bill remarks as we are finally leaving the pâtisserie, with three sandwiches and a half-eaten baguette (it arrived before the rest of the order). "Everyone wants to tell where they were when it happened." Haiti's earthquake, however, was such an overwhelming catastrophe; far more people died than even in the horrific earthquake and tsunami in Japan. But there is no need to compare tragedies; suffering is suffering, not any less intense if it's experienced by fewer casualties.

Still when the suffering is on such a colossal scale, it feels as if the world is destroyed, not just your corner of it. Did Haiti, not just Haitians, die in the earthquake? It's a wrenching question, which later I will come upon in Amy Wilentz's introduction to a new edition of *The Rainy Season*: "Is Haiti still here? . . . How many people can die in one event without destroying national identity? . . . Is a country a map, as we reflexively believe? What happens, then, when that map is erased?"

God's pencil has no eraser

W^e park across the street from the consulate, a two-story building that looks unscathed: no cracks on the walls, no pile of rubble in the yard. A Dominican flag droops on its pole on the roof. No need to keep waving chauvinistically above a destroyed city.

As we are disembarking, a black car pulls up to the entrance, and from its backseat emerges an officious woman in her thirties with a lot of attitude. You can tell — something cross about her expression, something big about her pocketbook, an extra umph in the slamming of the car door. I find myself hoping she does not work in the visa department.

The consulate personnel are busy as we enter. At a long counter, clerks are stamping visas in passports, stacking packets of them at one end. Business has been brisk: a lot of people wanting to go next door and wait out the devastation.

At a desk near the doorway, a young Dominican guy asks if he can help us.

"We're here to see Ruth Castro," I tell him. That's the name Señor Ortiz gave me over the phone. Ruth Castro at the consulate would receive us and help us resolve the problem with Piti's visa. "She's expecting us," I add, hoping to speed things up.

"You mean Ruffy Castor," the young man corrects me. So much for passing ourselves off as people she knows.

The guy is now looking us over: me, Bill, and Piti. But then, his eyes land on Mikaela, and he is instantly, visibly smitten. Daniel introduces himself and eagerly plies us with questions. What are we doing in Haiti? When will we be returning to the DR? He himself is headed home to Santo Domingo for the weekend, this very afternoon. Any chance we can meet up, anywhere we say? Mikaela glances over at me, and I know we are thinking the same thing: Is this the opportune time to tell Daniel that the day after tomorrow, she will be on an early morning flight home to DC?

Just then, there's a flurry of activity in the hallway: a woman is approaching, her progress impeded by petitioners needing a signature, an answer to a question, a problem solved. This must be Ruffy Castor, whom Daniel just buzzed. My heart sinks. It's the very woman I was hoping would not be taking care of us! Even without a big pocketbook and an automobile's door to bang shut, she still looks cross. Who knows what José Ortiz has told her about us.

"How can I help you?" Ruffy Castor asks, once we've introduced ourselves. Does she really not know? I'm wondering if José Ortiz did call her, after all.

Sheepishly, I explain that we need a visa for Piti. His old one, well, it expired a while ago. Again, I'm expecting a scolding, but Ruffy gets right to the point. "Let me see your passport," she asks Piti. Quickly, she reviews it; asks if we want a new visa for three months or for a year; collects the two-hundred-dollar fee for the year visa; tucks it inside the passport; then hands the packet over to one of the clerks to take care of. "It will be a few minutes," she explains. Meanwhile, she invites us to wait inside her office.

That's all there is to it? We're impressed. Give this woman a job running Marie Beliard!

We follow Ruffy down the hall and crowd into a minuscule office (so maybe she's not as important as I thought) with two chairs crammed on the other side of her large and cluttered desk. Bill and I sit, while Piti and Mikaela stand behind us. Once we're all packed in, Ruffy closes the door and turns on a rattling air conditioner — a little luxury, along with the chairs, she can offer us.

When we ask how long she has been in Haiti, Ruffy launches into her story about the earthquake. She was right here in her office; it was a little before five in the afternoon. She was already thinking of going home to her husband and her little six-month-old baby when the quake struck. She ran out on the street to find the world destroyed. All she could think of was her husband and child. Were they alive? Injured? She tried using her cell phone, but, of course, there was no reception. The anguish, the anguish she felt as she made her way home! It took her two hours on foot to reach her apartment, all the while passing scenes that kept stoking her terror. Thankfully, her husband and child were safe, her building still standing amid the surrounding rubble.

There is a knock on Ruffy's door: Piti's visa is ready. Bill asks Ruffy if there is anyone at the consulate we can hire to give us a tour of the city. It turns out there is a Haitian policeman assigned to the consulate, Leonard, whom she'd be happy to loan us. In parting, we exchange hugs. I recall my initial impression of Ruffy and wonder if I misjudged her, or if by listening to her story we gained access to a warmer, more caring person.

Before we proceed with Leonard to view the city, we stop at the Dominican embassy just a few blocks away. Ambassador Silié is currently at a conference in the Dominican Republic, but José Ortiz comes out of his office to greet us. A short, slender man with dark, expressive eyes, he is as gracious as Ruffy, though understandably a little wary at first. Every time we've been in touch in the past, it's with *problemas*.

But this time, we come with good news: Piti's visa issue has been resolved. And yes, we will be at the southern border crossing before five this afternoon.

I ask after his health. He looks to be in excellent shape, but since the earthquake, he has been very anxious, he explains. As he starts telling the story of that afternoon last January, his face tenses up. He was still at work when the earthquake struck, and although the embassy itself did not collapse, the next-door children's hospital fell on the portion of the building in which his office was located. He was trapped inside, unharmed but not knowing if any minute, in an aftershock, the roof would cave in and crush him. It was like being buried alive, he explains. The worst part was hearing the children screaming for help, and not being able to do anything for them. He was finally rescued, but the experience keeps playing over and over in his head.

As we leave the embassy, we are quiet, sobered by José's account. Months later, still preoccupied with the story he told us, I will e-mail him, asking if he knows what became of the children. Unfortunately, José does not.

Instead, he paints another haunting scene: panicked parents racing to the hospital to dig out their children. A few were carried away on stretchers to the makeshift clinics springing up around the city. But whether those made it, José cannot tell.

Inside the pickup, Leonard, our guide, begins recounting his own story. That January afternoon, he was standing at the gas station where he usually picks up his bus to go home at the end of the day. The first thing he heard was an eerie honking sound like an electric wire short-circuiting. Then he felt it: the earth undulating under his feet. He had to work hard to keep his balance. Leonard makes the honking sound over and over, so that finally I understand why people have named the earthquake *goudou goudou.*

"What would you like to see?" Leonard asks, after he finishes his story. We are on Pan American Avenue headed into downtown Port-au-Prince.

I have no idea what to ask for. In fact, I feel ashamed even making a selection. Let's see. Which scene of destruction and suffering will it be? As if we were ordering lunch from a menu at the Oloffson.

Bill wants to see the presidential palace — the enormous white confection that collapsed, its three domes deflated. I've seen it over and over in news footage. Hard to feel unalloyed sadness about the destruction of a structure that has housed so many scoundrels and self-serving public officials. But it is also a poor nation's proud monument. Tread softly, and throw away the big sticks.

The palace is a good choice. Leonard nods. Across from it there is a big tent city. As he directs us down to the city center, his cell phone rings. He is busy now, he tells the caller. But he can meet this person later. A journalist, he explains, once he gets off. Every time they come, they call him up. Back in January and February, there were many such calls, then they trickled off. But now again, with the six-month anniversary, the journalists are back. "I know what to show them," Leonard says. "And I offer protection." I'm reminded he is a policeman; his revolver sticks out at one hip from its holster. An armed Virgil in the ruined city.

We ride into the downtown area, full of ambivalence. To watch or not to watch. What is the respectful way to move through these scenes of devastation? We came to see, and according to Junior, Haiti needs to be seen. But something feels unsavory about visiting sites where people have suffered and are still suffering. You tell yourself you are here in solidarity. But at the end of the day, you add it up, and you still feel ashamed—at least I do. You haven't improved a damn thing. Natural disaster tourism—that's what it feels like.

But if that's all it is, the media has already brought us here and back without ever having to leave our homes. Everything we see gives us a sense of déjà vu: the palace crumpled as if a giant sat down on its roof; the tent cities where people are packed together in squalor with no place left to go; the children staring out listlessly from under tarps; women bathing themselves in the open, bathing their children, washing clothes, cooking on the sidewalk, stirring a row of steaming pots, smoke rising.

So what is it that the eye is seeking and the heart is aching for?

A flicker of wings, a thing that whispers hope. From a sidewalk wall hangs a red evening gown for sale. Incredible to think: there will be partying again! A boy in his school uniform walks by, holding the straps of his backpack. The very ordinariness of the moment seems a blessing.

On another sidewalk, an impromptu bookstore is spread out on top of a pile of rubble. The pickings are slim: *Bantu Philosophy*, a biography of Walt Disney, *150 Popular College Majors*. This, too, seems incredible: there will be reading again! College students will again be studying popular subjects, with a rare one reading up on Disney or the Bantus.

In front of a padlocked storefront, two young women are selling bouquets of plastic roses, blue and white, red and orange, wrapped in plastic. Somebody will buy them for a sweetheart's birthday, for a godchild's baptism, for a church altar. There will be occasions requiring floral punctuation again.

It's almost noon: a girls' school is letting out. The future women of Haiti pour out onto the streets, dressed in skirts of that beautiful sky-blue color and yellow blouses, with yellow bows in their hair. Mothers are again tying ribbons in their daughters' hair.

Meanwhile the tap-taps go by, urging us to love God, to love each other, to be thankful, to thank our mothers, to remember that all is possible. It seems a small miracle that we can still say these things to each other here.

There is a Kreyòl saying: God's pencil has no eraser. I've always understood the saying to mean that God doesn't need to erase. He makes no mistakes; his creation is perfect. But I now understand that saying in a more fatalistic way. There is no erasing or escaping the relentless march of events. And when that march tramples your loved ones or plays havoc in your part of the world (whether Haiti, Chile, New Zealand, Japan, or our own USA), you do what you have to do: you mourn, you bury your dead, you get up the next day and cook for the ones who are left, braid hair, sing songs, tell stories. Somehow you get through. As for the rest of us, we look; we listen; we try to help — even when it seems there is nothing we can do.

The one thing we cannot do is turn away. For our humanity also does not have the eraser option. When we have seen a thing, we have an obligation. To see and to allow ourselves to be transformed by what we have seen.

Later, I will ask Bill why he wanted to see Port-au-Prince. Didn't he feel a little like a motorist who stops to gawk at an accident? "I would have if I was just going there for myself. But now we have Piti. It was important for him to see it and for us to be with him when he did." (Yes, reader, this is the same guy who had to sleep at the

Oloffson. I sometimes seem to forget: you get all the parts when you love a whole person.)

Periodically, as we drive around, I turn to check on Piti and Mikaela. Both are big-eyed, subdued by the magnitude of the devastation. Piti's face is that of the grave old man who seems to be showing up more often lately. But every once in a while, when I point out the red evening gown, when I tease that one day one of those young schoolgirls in uniform with yellow ribbons will be Ludy, his face lights up, the face of that grinning boy of long ago with a homemade kite he was getting ready to fly.

He, too, is being transformed by what he is seeing. In the months following this trip to Port-au-Prince, Piti will reactivate a support group Eli helped found for Haitians working at Alta Gracia and on surrounding farms. Piti will name it CJM, Cooperative des Jeunes de Moustique, Young People of Moustique Cooperative, and redefine its mission from one of just helping each other, to one of working toward the future of Haiti. The cooperative will elect Piti president. From laborer to *capataz* to president of CJM. God's blessings are raining down on him, as Piti tells me, for a reason. What that is, he hopes to find out.

But one thing he does know: Haiti is not erased. It is alive in his imagination and in ours. Haiti is what cannot be erased in a human being, not with slavery, not with centuries of exploitation and bad management, invasions, earthquakes, hurricanes, cholera. It embodies those undervalued but increasingly valuable skills we will need to survive on this slowly depleting planet: endurance, how to live with less, how to save by sharing, how to make a pact with hope when you find yourself in hell. The poet Philip Booth once wrote, "How you get there is where you'll arrive." How we respond to Haiti is perhaps more critical than we imagine: a preview of where we are likely to end up as a human family.

One last critical survival skill

After two hours of driving around, Leonard directs us to the road that will lead us out of the city to the border. He himself will get out here and take a motorcycle taxi to his meeting with the journalist.

How can he bear to do this again? Leonard shrugs. Actually, he is grateful to God for the extra income he is earning. He has been able to help his extended family and friends rebuild their lives. There is money to be made in the ruined city — not just in high-end hotels and restaurants.

And not all of this money ends up lining a full pocket. Some of it helps fill an empty stomach.

As we drive away from the city center, I remind Bill about lunch. "You know, at the Oloffson?" I say it matter-of-factly. All grievance has washed out of me. What is left is a great, familiar tiredness at the ways we keep failing each other.

"I'm not hungry," Bill murmurs. He, too, feels chastened, I can tell.

The road to the border is a breeze. It's the main artery between the two countries; the one politicos use when they are deposed and the Toussaint L'Ouverture Airport is closed; the road that big transport trucks travel, bringing in supplies from the Dominican Republic and taking back undocumented Haitian workers; the road that four weary, heavyhearted travelers are now on, headed home, all of us too overcome to have much to talk about.

As we are leaving Haiti, I look out my window, and there, beside an excavated mountainside, two stone slabs rise out of a pile of rubble like hands steepled together in prayer. Haiti is still speaking to me. I had forgotten our conversation.

By the time we cross the border, evening is coming on. It's a long drive north to Santiago from this southern entry point, so we decide to spend the night at a small seaside hotel. At supper, Bill asks Piti if he'll play some songs for us and the other patrons at the restaurant. We're all feeling raw after the day in Port-au-Prince, hoping for a repeat of the magical night in Moustique.

But it doesn't happen, which surprises me. You'd think Piti's gospel songs would appeal to the group of eighteen

missionaries sitting at a long table in the middle of the restaurant. They've just arrived from a small town in Geor-
gia to repair a church on the border they built six years
ago. Not one turns his chair around. Not one sings along.
Not one gets up to dance.

If not here, I find myself hoping, let it be happening
back in Haiti. Let there be another free concert going on
outside one of the tent cities. Let someone wear that red
dress and dance to the sounds of a famous band, maybe
RAM. Let there be singing and dancing again, even if it
keeps someone awake all night or causes a fight.

Back in our room, Bill and I get ready for bed. Through
the open window, we can hear the waves crashing on the
cliffs, a sound that always makes me think of Matthew Ar-
nold's "Dover Beach," a poem I so loved in college I learned
it by heart and can still recite it. In the poem, a man is listening to the ocean at night, and a wave of despair washes
over him. All he can hear in its grating roar is "the ebb and
flow of human misery." The world seems a darkling plain
without joy or certitude or help of pain. In the final lines,
overcome by an apocalyptic vision, which has to be one of
the bleakest in English poetry, he calls his beloved to the
window. "Ah love, let us be true to one another," he begs
her. That much they can posit together.

"Are you feeling a little better?" I ask tentatively, because it is and it isn't the question I want to ask.

"A lot better, especially after that supper."

Any further inroads into trying to mend fences feels premature. And so, not knowing what to say, I say too much: "Would you marry me again if you had it to do over?"

Bill turns to me, his face in a scowl, as if I've asked the most ridiculous question in the world. "What do you mean? You're my life."

I'm almost in tears with gratitude to him for being able to see me clearly, and still love me—another critical survival skill I'm struggling to learn. "But it gets so rough some times!"

"No it doesn't," Bill pronounces. And this time I am so glad for his sturdy certitude, I keep my mouth shut. On this rock I have built my marriage.

Back in his own room, Piti is strumming his guitar. I wonder if he is missing Eseline and Ludy on this, his first night away from Haiti.

He has no way of knowing that within a month, they will be back, having crossed over with Wilson. Eseline will be feeling fine, happy to be coming home to her husband and little house. Meanwhile, Ludy will be walking, reaching for everything, putting it in her mouth. (Oh dear,

how to babyproof a humble *casita*?) She will also be talking a blue streak, saying *ma-ma, pa-pa*, making those non-
sense syllables that sound eerily like *goudou, goudou*, but
refer only to the wonders she is seeing and learning to name
in this world.